# work**skills**™
## Reading

### PROGRAM CONSULTANTS

Bonnie Goonen

Susan Pittman-Shetler

Steck-Vaughn®

HOUGHTON MIFFLIN HARCOURT

www.steckvaughn.com/adulted
800-289-4490

Photo Acknowledgements:
P. cover ©Photoalto/SuperStock; 4 (c), 12–13 ©Radius Images/Alamy; 5 ©Siede Preis/Photodisc/Getty Images;
34–35 ©Real World People/Alamy; 4 (tl), 72–73 ©Brownstock Inc./Alamy; 4, (bl), 110–111 ©Monty Rakusen/Cultura/
Getty Images; 140–141 ©Mike Kemp/Getty Images.

Printed in the U.S.A.

ISBN   978-0-547-53659-0

3 4 5 6 7 8 9 10   1689    20 19 18 17 16 15 14 13 12 11

4500298569        A B C D E F G

# Table of Contents

Welcome to Steck-Vaughn's *WorkSkills*™    4

Pretest Assessment (Online)

**Chapter 1**   **Determine the Reading Purpose**

    **Lesson 1:** Workplace Texts    14

    **Lesson 2:** Define the Purpose/Main Idea    22

    **Skills for the Workplace:** Identify the Source    30

    Chapter 1 Assessment    32

**Chapter 2**   **Use Reading Strategies**

    **Lesson 3:** Preview Workplace Documents    36

    **Lesson 4:** Preview Graphic Displays    44

    **Lesson 5:** Understand Sequence    52

    **Lesson 6:** Make Predictions    60

    **Skills for the Workplace:** Identify Text Features    68

    Chapter 2 Assessment    70

**Chapter 3**   **Check and Enhance Comprehension**

    **Lesson 7:** Main Idea and Supporting Details    74

    **Lesson 8:** Use Context Clues    82

    **Lesson 9:** Understand Signs and Visuals    90

    **Lesson 10:** Summarize    98

    **Skills for the Workplace:** Note Taking    106

    Chapter 3 Assessment    108

**Chapter 4**   **Analyze Information**

    **Lesson 11:** Make Inferences    112

    **Lesson 12:** Identify Cause and Effect    120

    **Lesson 13:** Compare and Contrast    128

    **Skills for the Workplace:** Fact and Opinion    136

    Chapter 4 Assessment    138

**Chapter 5**   **Integrate New Information with Prior Knowledge**

    **Lesson 14:** Apply Information to a New Context    142

    **Lesson 15:** Synthesize Information from Multiple Sources    150

    **Skills for the Workplace:** Workplace Jargon    158

    Chapter 5 Assessment    160

OFFICIAL Work Readiness Practice Test (Online)

*WorkSkills*™ Glossary    162

Answers and Explanations    164

= Online Assessments

# Welcome to Steck-Vaughn's *WorkSkills*™

## Setting Yourself Apart in Today's Job Market

You probably already know that finding the right job for you can be a time-consuming and sometimes difficult process. You may have to sort through hundreds of job listings in order to find the few that seem right for your skills and experience.

The same is true for employers. A manager may receive hundreds or even thousands of applications for only a few open positions. How can you make yourself stand out as one of the best applicants for the job?

When looking for entry-level workers, employers want to be assured that a new employee has the knowledge and skills that he or she needs in order to be successful. Many of the skills that can help you stand out to a potential employer are also skills that you use every day. Have you ever:

- read or written an e-mail?
- estimated whether you had enough money to buy something?
- resolved a conflict with a friend or family member?
- spoken with a technical support person to solve a problem with your cell phone or computer?

If so, then you have used skills that employers value and that will help you succeed in finding and keeping a job.

Steck-Vaughn's *WorkSkills*™ is designed to assist you in identifying these skills and **developing your strengths** in these areas. Together with the **National Work Readiness Credential**, *WorkSkills*™ helps you prove to potential employers that **you are ready for a great career!**

## What Can the National Work Readiness Credential Do for You?

Some skills are specific to a particular job. If you work in construction, you probably don't need to know how to operate a cash register. However, there are other skills that apply to almost every job. The National Work Readiness Council has worked with employers in many fields to identify the knowledge, skills, and abilities needed by entry-level employees. These skills fall into four main categories:

- **Communication Skills:** reading with understanding, listening actively, speaking clearly, and thinking critically

- **Interpersonal Skills:** cooperating with others, negotiating, resolving conflicts, and giving and receiving support

- **Decision-Making Skills:** identifying and solving problems (including some that require math), making decisions, and planning ahead

- **Lifelong Learning Skills:** taking responsibility for your own learning, identifying your strengths and weaknesses, and being willing and motivated to learn new skills

Earning the National Work Readiness Credential shows employers that you have these skills. It also shows that you are motivated, have a strong work ethic, and are willing to take initiative. These qualities will set you apart from many other people who are applying for the same jobs that you are. The National Work Readiness Credential gives you an edge by showing employers that you have what it takes to succeed on the job.

To earn the National Work Readiness Credential, you will need to take and pass four separate tests:

- **Reading**

- **Math**

- **Situational Judgment**

- **Active Listening**

# Prove Your Potential with *WorkSkills*™

The *WorkSkills*™ series is designed to provide you with the instruction and practice you need to master the National Work Readiness Credential assessment. This series will help you make progress toward your career goals. The *WorkSkills*™ books focus on applying reading, math, listening and speaking, and interpersonal skills in real-world workplace scenarios. In these books, all of the skills and strategies you learn will be taught in the context of real workplace scenarios, the kinds of situations that you will encounter on the job. Each lesson will teach the strategy, show you how to apply it, and then give you lots of examples that allow you to practice applying the skill or strategy to real workplace situations.

## Consistent Lesson Structure Enhances Mastery

Every lesson in the *WorkSkills*™ series uses the same format. This uniform structure enables you to gradually master each skill.

### Build on What You Know

This section introduces the skills by making connections to your daily life or in the workplace. The Essential Skills that you will be learning are clearly identified on the first page of the lesson. The "In Real Life" features connect and apply these skills to workplace scenarios.

### Develop Your Skills

This section provides in-depth instruction on the skills or strategies that are the focus of the lesson. Examples illustrate how to apply skills and strategies in workplace situations, and questions guide you through the steps you will use to successfully apply these strategies on your own. The "Got It?" feature summarizes the key points you should remember from each lesson.

### Apply Your Knowledge

Practice the skills and strategies you have learned. A "To Do List" gives you a reminder of key points and processes, while another "In Real Life" scenario provides an opportunity to take what you have learned and apply it to another workplace scenario. "Think About It!" gives you a chance to reflect on what you have learned and the different ways that you can use it in the workplace.

### Test Your WRC Skills

Each lesson concludes with a *Test Your WRC Skills* section. These pages use questions modeled after those you will see on the National Work Readiness Credential assessment to give you practice applying the skills you have learned. Answers are provided at the back of the book.

## Assessments

The *WorkSkills*™ series includes a number of tools to help you assess what you already know, identify the skill areas on which you may need to focus, and monitor your progress as you study. As you have seen, the lessons include a number of opportunities for you to use what you know and what you are learning in real-world applications of important workplace skills. In addition, there are several other opportunities, both within the books and online, for you to practice applying your skills by answering questions that are similar to those you will see on the National Work Readiness Credential assessment.

### Online Pretests

Before you begin your studies in this book, take the Online Pretest, which is a full-length practice version of the National Work Readiness Credential assessment. The questions on the Pretest mimic those on the National Work Readiness Credential assessment in style, format, and content.

### Chapter Assessments

#### Student Book Chapter Assessments

At the end of each chapter in the book, questions similar to those on the National Work Readiness Credential assessment allow you to determine whether you have mastered the Essential Skills that you learned in the chapter.

#### Additional Online Chapter Assessments

The Online Chapter Assessments allow you to evaluate your mastery of the skills taught in the chapter you have just completed, as well as skills taught in previous chapters of the book. The questions are similar in style to those you will see on the National Work Readiness Credential assessment.

### Online OFFICIAL Work Readiness Practice Tests

The Online OFFICIAL Work Readiness Practice Tests are the full-length practice version of the National Work Readiness Credential assessment and are endorsed by the National Work Readiness Council. Use your results to assess what you have learned and where additional study may be needed.

### Answers and Explanations

You can quickly check your answers for each student book Chapter Assessment question, as well as the *Test Your WRC Skills* sections, in the *Answers and Explanations* section in the back of the book. This feature provides the correct answer, as well as a full explanation for why each answer choice is correct or incorrect. When taking the Online Chapter Assessments, you will get automated feedback.

Today's adult education and workforce development programs face significant challenges in adequately preparing adults for entry into the workplace. However, the National Work Readiness Council has issued a new credential based on the *Equipped for the Future* standards. According to the NWRC, the new National Work Readiness Credential assessment assists educational professionals in:

- Assessing a learner's skills and needs.

- Creating learning experiences based on a simple standard of integrated skills and tasks.

- Providing competency goals that are useful for instruction and aspirational for learners.

- Aligning instruction to a standard defined by business.

- Demonstrating performance outcomes to funding organizations.

> " Getting and keeping a job is an important first step to meeting the demands of adulthood and self-sufficiency. "
>
> —Joe Mizereck,
> Acting Executive Director of the
> National Work Readiness Council

The National Work Readiness Credential assessment is designed to assess a worker's on-the-job skills in four areas: reading, math, situational judgment, and active listening.

## Steck-Vaughn's *WorkSkills*™ Series

If adult education and workforce development programs are to prepare students to pass the National Work Readiness Credential assessment, they need material that assists them in making the connection between what they learn in the classroom and how they can use that information in the workplace. Steck-Vaughn's *WorkSkills*™ series is designed to prepare adult learners to successfully pass the National Work Readiness Credential assessment and earn the National Work Readiness Credential. The series has been designed to cover all Domains and Essential Tasks, as identified by the National Work Readiness Council. Mastery of these tasks is viewed as necessary for adults to effectively be prepared for entry-level positions.

**Steck-Vaughn's *WorkSkills*™ is endorsed by the**

## Benefits That Set *WorkSkills*™ Apart

- Contextualized and integrated instruction
- Focus on real-world, workplace contexts and skills
- Gradual-release model of modeling-practice-application-test
- Written for non-traditional learners: approachable tone and accessible format
- Controlled readability, ranging from 7.0–8.9
- Print, online, and audio components
- Assessments that mimic the actual National Work Readiness Credential assessment:
  - Online Pretests
  - Online OFFICIAL Work Readiness Practice Tests
  - Chapter Assessments (available in print and online)
  - *Test Your WRC Skills* sections
- Answer keys with explanations/solutions
- Workplace Glossary

## Components of the *WorkSkills*™ series include:

### Available in Print

*WorkSkills*™ Reading

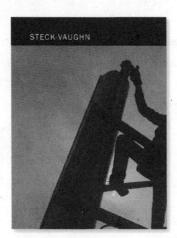

*WorkSkills*™ Math

*WorkSkills*™ Situational Judgment and Active Listening

### Available Online

- Online Pretests
- Downloadable Scenarios/Audio Scripts for Active Listening
- Additional Chapter Assessment questions

- Online OFFICIAL Work Readiness Practice Tests
- Online Teacher Lessons, available as printable PDFs

**For online assessments and instructor support, visit www.mysteckvaughn.com/WORK.**

# Steck-Vaughn's *WorkSkills*™ Reading

All three books in the *WorkSkills*™ series have been designed to address the Work Readiness Domains and Essential Tasks. The *WorkSkills*™ Reading book has been organized so that each chapter represents one of the five Reading Domains. Within each chapter, Essential Tasks are the focus for each lesson.

I. Determine the Reading Purpose

II. Use Reading Strategies Appropriate to the Purpose

III. Check and Enhance Comprehension of What Was Read

IV. Analyze the Information and Reflect on Its Underlying Meaning

V. Integrate New Information with Prior Knowledge to Address the Reading Purpose

## Reading Strategies for the Workplace

This book teaches students the strategies they can use for successful reading on the job. Each lesson teaches a strategy, models how to apply it, and then gives numerous examples so students can practice applying the strategy in the context of workplace documents.

## Real-World Workplace Documents

The use of graphics, such as charts, forms, and signs, is common in the workplace. Therefore, much of the material in the National Work Readiness Credential assessment is presented in a graphic format. To provide students ample opportunities to build the skills necessary to interpret and use different types of graphic-based materials, *WorkSkills*™ Reading includes a heavy emphasis on graphic materials, including the following workplace documents:

- Work schedule
- Dress code
- Safety sign
- Fire-drill procedure
- E-mail
- Order form
- Employee manual
- Instructions
- Meeting agenda
- Announcement
- Return policy
- Memo

# Workforce Readiness
## Real World. Real Skills.

## The *WorkSkills*™ Reading Lesson at a Glance

**Essential Tasks**

Each chapter focuses on one Work Readiness Domain, and each lesson focuses on critical Essential Tasks.

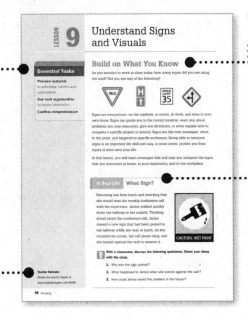

**Controlled Readability**

The readability of instruction is controlled, averaging between 7.0–8.9.

**Real-World Workplace Documents**

Students practice applying reading strategies in the context of real workplace documents.

**Online Teacher Lessons**

The online teacher lessons, available as printable PDFs, provide instructors with strategies and activities to help students master reading skills.

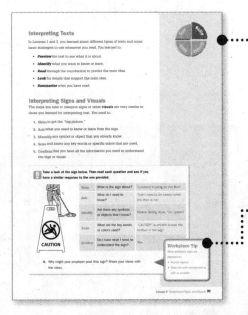

**Four-Step Process**

The gradual-release model of instruction enables learners to Build, Develop, and Apply new skills. Then learners Test their skills to assess their understanding.

**Workplace Tips**

These examples and helpful tips enable students to apply what they learn in the lesson to the workplace.

## Purchase the
## National Work Readiness Credential assessment

Steck-Vaughn has proudly partnered with the National Work Readiness Council to be the exclusive distributor of the National Work Readiness Credential assessment. Contact your sales representative for more details. You may also contact our customer service team at **800-289-4490** or visit our website at **www.steckvaughn.com/adulted**.

# CHAPTER 1

# Determine the Reading Purpose

What kinds of texts are you likely to encounter in the workplace? How and why are they used? In this chapter, you will learn the answers to these questions by interacting with several types of workplace documents and identifying the purpose and audience for each document type.

# Workplace Texts

## Essential Tasks

**Identify work-related expectations** associated with the reading task

**Use text format and features** to find specific information

## Build on What You Know

On a typical workday, what types of documents do you think you might read, and why? Outside of work, texts such as e-mail and text messages help you to stay informed and keep in touch with peers. Workplace texts also help you do this. However, they are specially designed to help you do your job.

No matter where you work, you are expected to read and understand job-related **documents**. Memos, manuals, agendas, policies, and other types of texts help workers stay organized, on task, and safe.

In this lesson, you will learn about some of the texts you'll encounter in the workplace. You will also learn some basic **strategies** to help you better understand these texts.

## Getting Started

When you receive a document in the workplace, what do you do? In most cases, it's a good idea to review the materials as soon as you can. The following strategies will help you understand a workplace document, one step at a time.

When you receive a document at work, you should:

- *Preview* the text to see what it is about. Are there titles or images that help you know what the document is about?

- *Identify* what you want to know or learn. Is the document a memo, an order form, or some kind of instructions? Knowing what kind of document you are looking at will help you understand its purpose.

- *Read* through the introduction to predict the main idea. Read carefully for key words and clues that help you identify the main idea.

- *Look* for details that support the main idea, including pictures or charts. Are there images that help clarify information in the document?

- *Summarize* what you have read. Understanding the document's main idea will help you know what action to take next.

You can use these strategies throughout this book to help you better understand what you read.

**Teacher Reminder**
Review the teacher lesson at
www.mysteckvaughn.com/WORK

## Where and When?

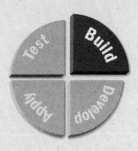

Maria was recently hired on as a cashier at a clothing store. She received the following work schedule.

| TIME | Mon. | Tues. | Wed. | Thurs. | Fri. | Sat. | Sun. |
|------|------|-------|------|--------|------|------|------|
| 9:00–3:00 | Maria | Maria | Sam | Sam | Maria | Maria | Closed |
| 3:00–10:00 | Sam | Sam | Maria | Maria | Sam | Sam | Closed |

 **Take a look at the work schedule and discuss the following questions with a classmate.**

1. What information can you get from a work schedule?

2. How is this schedule similar to or different from schedules you have used?

3. What other types of jobs do you think require a work schedule?

4. What is a benefit of having a schedule?

## Different Types of Workplace Documents

As you've learned, a work schedule is a straightforward way of letting you know when you're expected at work. Once you arrive at work, you will probably encounter several other kinds of documents.

For example, if you are starting a new job, your employer may provide you with an employee manual. This manual will offer an overview of your job. It will also include company policies you are expected to know and follow. It may even provide instructions that help you complete particular tasks on the job. It is important that you closely read manuals, instructions, and policies. Understanding these resources will help you excel at your job.

Depending on your line of work, you may also read agendas, memos, flyers, and order forms. In this lesson, you will learn about each of these types of documents and its purpose in the workplace.

Fortunately, workplace documents are intended to be clear and informative. Once you learn to identify each type and understand its purpose, reading texts in the workplace will become second nature.

> **Workplace Tip**
>
> Most workplace documents are intended to:
> - Answer questions you may have about your job.
> - Provide information that helps you reach your goals in the workplace.

# Develop Your Skills

Understanding workplace documents is an important part of your job. The following activities will help you identify and understand some of the kinds of documents you will likely encounter at work.

## What's on the Agenda?

An agenda is similar to a to-do list you might use outside of work. It shows what must be discussed or addressed, and in what order.

For example, Peter works as a restaurant host. The restaurant manager has called a meeting to discuss each employee's responsibilities. She distributed the following meeting agenda.

 **Review the agenda and answer the following questions.**

1. Why do you think the manager created a meeting agenda?

2. Why do you think questions and concerns are saved for last?

3. Have you ever received an agenda for a meeting? If so, how was the agenda helpful?

> **Meeting Agenda**
>
> 6/28/2012
> Main Dining Room
> Attendees: All restaurant staff
>
> I.   Roll Call
> II.  New Sections of Restaurant
> III. New Responsibilities
>      A. Wait Staff
>      B. Hosts
>      C. Managers
> IV.  Questions and Concerns

## The Best Policy

Policies, instructions, and manuals provide specific information and guidelines that employees should follow.

For example, Javier works for a construction company. In his employee manual, he received a dress code policy that he must follow.

**Review the dress code policy and discuss the questions with a classmate.**

4. Why might a construction company enforce a dress code?

5. Have you ever had to follow a dress code? If so, why?

6. What other types of businesses do you think have dress codes, and why?

> **B&A Construction
> Company Dress Code**
>
> **Office:**
> · Khaki pants
> · Company-issued shirt
> · Dress shoes or loafers
>
> **Job Site:**
> · Company-issued uniform, including shirt and pants
> · Steel-toed boots
>
> Employees are expected to wear their name badges at all times.

**Workplace Tip**

Paying close attention to each item on an agenda can help you organize your thoughts and any questions you may have.

# Place Your Order

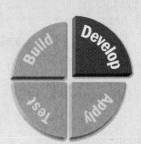

An order form is a document a customer uses to request merchandise from a company. After receiving payment for the merchandise, the company uses the form to make sure the customer receives what he or she ordered.

For example, Nora works for an athletic wear company. When customers order merchandise online or by mail, Nora is responsible for processing their order forms and making sure their orders ship on time.

 **Review the sample order form and answer the following questions with a classmate.**

## Old Varsity Athletics

| Item Number | Description | Size | Quantity | Price* (each) |
|---|---|---|---|---|
| 124756 | black shorts | M | 2 | $15.00 |
| 193423 | red shirt | M | 4 | $12.00 |
| 849372 | shoes | 10.5 | 1 | $60.00 |

*Tax included on all purchases

| | |
|---|---|
| Shipping | $8.00 |
| Total | $146.00 |

**7.** How many shirts did the customer order?

**8.** What other information can be found on this order form?

**9.** What steps do you think Nora should take after receiving this order form?

---

**GOT IT?** Identify each of the texts you've learned about so far. When reading a workplace document, remember to:

- Preview the text to see what it is about.

- Identify what you want to learn and read the document carefully.

- Read for key words and clues that help you understand the main idea.

- Look for images that help clarify information in the document.

- Summarize what you have read so you know what action to take next.

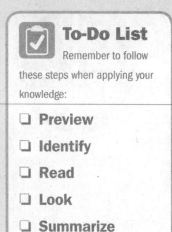

**To-Do List**

Remember to follow these steps when applying your knowledge:

❏ **Preview**

❏ **Identify**

❏ **Read**

❏ **Look**

❏ **Summarize**

# Apply Your Knowledge

Use the reading strategies you learned earlier in the lesson to identify and understand the purpose of a document in the workplace.

**Read each of the following scenarios and its accompanying document. Select the correct answer for each question.**

1. Colin recently started a job with a painting company. He and his fellow employees received the following memo about an upcoming job.

> **To:** Employees
> **From:** Management
> **Re:** Respiratory masks
>
> This memo is to inform employees of a safety concern on an upcoming job. Due to poor ventilation at Lakes Market, all employees will be required to wear respiratory masks while working inside the building. Your supervisor will distribute these masks on 11/19.
>
> Thank you for your cooperation, and please see your supervisor with concerns.

**Based on the memo, Colin should:**

A. Purchase a respiratory mask as soon as possible.

B. Work only near doors and windows at Lakes Market.

C. See his supervisor on 11/19 to pick up his respiratory mask.

D. Find out whether Lakes Market sells respiratory masks.

2. What other purposes might a memo serve in the workplace?

3. Eve noticed the following flyer in her office's break room:

> **Help keep the office healthy this flu season!**
>
> FREE flu shots on 9/1, from 12:00 until 2:00

**Why might a company post this flyer?**

A. To remind employees to make appointments to see their doctors

B. To help keep employees healthy and productive

C. To remind employees that flu season is coming

D. To outline an important policy for employees

4. Amitra works for a furniture manufacturer. Her job is to stain and finish furniture after it is built. Her supervisor handed out the following guidelines.

---

### Help Maintain a Clean Work Environment

1. Properly clean or dispose of containers that held paint, stain, or other chemicals.

2. Fold and stack all drop cloths.

3. Clean brushes and rollers with soap and water.

4. Sweep workstation and dispose of any trash.

---

**Why might Amitra's employer distribute these guidelines?**

**A.** So employees will throw away old drop cloths

**B.** To remind employees that filthy workstations lead to accidents

**C.** So employees will make room for new furniture in their workstations

**D.** To remind employees to keep clean, safe workstations

---

## In Real Life | Put Your Skills to Work!

You work as a security guard at a large office building. A number of cars have been broken into or vandalized recently, and it's your job to help find a solution. You and your supervisor decide that on-duty guards should tour the parking lot more often. You also come up with a system for quickly reporting suspicious activity. Your supervisor has asked you to alert the other guards about these issues.

 **Think about the problem you are facing and put your skills to work! What kind of document should you create to alert your fellow guards? What information should you include? Explain your answers.**

### Workplace Tip

When deciding what type of document to create, think about:

- The purpose of the document
- Which information is most important
- How your document should be organized

## Think About It!

**In the line of work you hope to pursue, what kinds of documents do you think you'll read on a typical workday?**

Being able to predict the kinds of texts you might encounter on the job will help you prepare for understanding them. Remember, workplace texts tell you important information about your job. Knowing how to use the reading strategies introduced in this lesson will help you understand the various documents you encounter in the workplace.

**Answer Key**

1. C

2. Answers will vary.

3. B

4. D

# Test Your WRC Skills

**Understanding workplace documents requires a variety of reading skills. Read the scenarios and review each document. Select the answer you think best responds to the question.**

**1.** According to the memo, what should all mail carriers be sure to do?

---

**Memo**

**To:** Mail Carriers

**From:** Management

**Date:** 12/14/2012

**Re:** Stormy Conditions

This memo is to address recent weather activity that has affected mail delivery. Stormy weather and poor road conditions have caused many mail carriers to fall behind on their routes. To solve this problem, we are shortening routes and sending out additional carriers to help ensure prompt delivery of mail.

Your supervisor will distribute temporary new routes on 12/15/2012. Please prepare for stormy weather by dressing warmly.

---

**A.** ○ Split their mail routes with additional carriers.

**B.** ○ Work faster to ensure prompt delivery of mail.

**C.** ○ Prepare for stormy weather by dressing warmly.

**D.** ○ Tell their supervisors to shorten all mail routes.

**2.** Read the following excerpt from your company's holiday pay policy. What happens if you agree to work on a paid holiday?

---

Employees who agree to work on a paid holiday will receive regular pay plus holiday pay. Holiday pay will not be paid if:

1. The employee has been with the company for fewer than 90 days.
2. The employee is a temporary or seasonal employee.
3. The employee is asked to work on a paid holiday and refuses to do so.
4. The employee is on leave or on lay-off status.

---

**A.** ○ You are considered a seasonal employee.

**B.** ○ You receive holiday pay instead of your regular pay.

**C.** ○ You will be allowed to take a leave of absence.

**D.** ○ You receive holiday pay plus your regular pay.

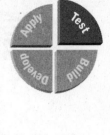

**3.** How many days is Manuel required to work, according to this schedule?

| TIME | Mon. | Tues. | Wed. | Thurs. | Fri. | Sat. | Sun. |
|------|------|-------|------|--------|------|------|------|
| 9:00–5:00 | Manuel | Manuel | Gus | Gus | Sue | Sue | Manuel |
| 2:00–10:00 | Sue | Sue | Manuel | Manuel | Gus | Ruth | Gus |

A. ○ 4
B. ○ 5
C. ○ 6
D. ○ 7

**4.** You have been hired to assist a pharmacist. The following checklist outlines your duties. What are you responsible for?

> ___Receive supplies and medication deliveries.
> ___Unpack and label incoming items.
> ___Prepare and maintain inventory records.
> ___Compile and file inventory and prescription records.
> ___Prepare and type prescription labels.

A. ○ Unpacking prescription labels
B. ○ Preparing all medication deliveries
C. ○ Sorting incoming items
D. ○ Filing inventory and prescription records

**5.** According to this section of an order form, which item did the customer order the most of?

| Item Number | Description | Size | Quantity | Price (each) |
|-------------|-------------|------|----------|--------------|
| 124756 | khaki pants | M | 4 | $45.00 |
| 193423 | blue blazer | M | 2 | $80.00 |
| 849372 | black shoes | 12 | 1 | $75.00 |
| 758321 | striped tie | N/A | 3 | $20.00 |

A. ○ Khaki pants
B. ○ Blue blazer
C. ○ Black shoes
D. ○ Striped tie

Check your answers on page 164.

# Define the Purpose/ Main Idea

## Build on What You Know

Whether you read a text at home or at work, understanding its **purpose** and main idea is essential. Documents you read outside of work serve a number of purposes. Some entertain. Others inform or instruct. Similarly, each type of workplace document you've learned about also has a specific purpose.

For example, when you receive a memo at work, you may already know that the purpose of a memo is to make an announcement, bring attention to a problem, or resolve a conflict. Knowing the purpose helps you as you read to find the document's main idea. When you understand the main idea of a memo or other workplace document, you will know what action to take next.

Throughout this lesson, you will learn and apply reading strategies to understand the purpose and main idea of various workplace documents.

### In Real Life    A Change of Plans

To prepare for a busy day, Sonia has made a list of tasks she must complete before a company-wide meeting. After finishing her list, she receives the following e-mail from her supervisor.

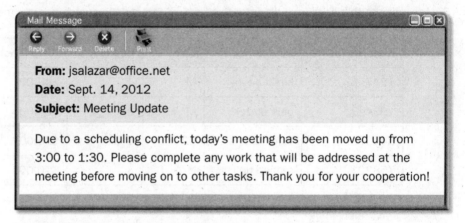

Mail Message

**From:** jsalazar@office.net
**Date:** Sept. 14, 2012
**Subject:** Meeting Update

Due to a scheduling conflict, today's meeting has been moved up from 3:00 to 1:30. Please complete any work that will be addressed at the meeting before moving on to other tasks. Thank you for your cooperation!

 **Discuss the following questions. Share your ideas with the class.**

1. What is the purpose of this e-mail?

2. How might Sonia need to adjust her to-do list based on this e-mail?

3. What might happen if Sonia didn't read or understand this e-mail?

# Using Reading Strategies

To help you determine the purpose and main idea of a text, remember to use the following strategies:

- *Preview* What basic information can you gather at a glance? Look for titles, headings, and images that help you determine a text's purpose.

- *Identify* What kind of document are you reading? For example, is it a memo, schedule, manual, or order form? Knowing what kind of document you are reading will help you quickly identify its purpose.

- *Read* Are there key words or clues in the introduction that help you identify the main idea of the text?

- *Look* Are there details such as images, graphs, or charts that provide information about the document? As you read, these images may clarify information and help you understand the main idea of the text.

- *Summarize* Can you briefly say what the text is about or what action is required? When you summarize a text, you restate its main idea.

 **Use the strategies above as you read the following memo. Then read each question and discuss possible answers with a classmate.**

---

### Memo

**To:** Employees of Mason's Electronics

**From:** Management

**Date:** November 20, 2012

**Re:** Holiday Schedule

This memo is a reminder that the holidays are the busiest time of year at Mason's Electronics. As a result, we will require extra help in Customer Service and with stocking throughout the month of December.

Any employees who volunteer to work overtime this month will receive overtime compensation, as well as an increased employee discount at the store. A sign-up sheet has been posted in the break room. Please sign up by November 25 for any additional shifts you plan to work.

See store management with any questions or concerns. Thank you!

---

4. What is the main idea of this memo?

5. What words or phrases in the first paragraph help you guess the main idea of the memo?

6. How would you summarize this memo?

# Develop Your Skills

In the following activities, you will learn reading strategies to determine the purpose and main idea of different kinds of workplace documents.

## Preview and Identify for Purpose

Previewing will help you identify the type of document you are reading and what it is about. Knowing what kind of document you are reading will help you determine its purpose.

For example, Diego is a hotel clerk. He received the work schedule below.

| TIME | Mon. | Tues. | Wed. | Thurs. | Fri. | Sat. | Sun. |
|---|---|---|---|---|---|---|---|
| 9:00–5:00 | Diego | Diego | Kim | Kim | Paul | Paul | Ruth |
| 12:00–8:00 | Paul | Paul | Diego | Diego | Kim | Ruth | Kim |
| 5:00–1:00 | Kim | Kim | Paul | Paul | Ruth | Diego | Diego |

 **Review the work schedule and answer the following questions.**

1. What is the purpose of this work schedule?

2. Who would find the schedule useful?

## Read for Main Idea

After you preview and identify the purpose of a document, read closely for key words and phrases that help you determine the main idea.

For example, Meghan works as a tile setter. She received the following instructions for an upcoming job.

| General Instructions for Tile Setters |
|---|

1. Carefully measure the area.
2. Determine how many tiles will be required.
3. Plan for areas where tiles need to be cut or shaped around obstacles.

4. Make sure cutting tools, grout, and all other tools and safety equipment are at the job site.
5. Carefully work with a partner to complete assigned areas.

 **Review the instructions and discuss the questions with a classmate.**

3. What is the purpose of these instructions?

4. Why do you think the word *carefully* is repeated?

5. What key words or phrases help you understand the main idea of the instructions?

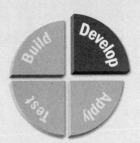

# Look for Details That Support the Main Idea

You know that key words and phrases help you determine the main idea of a text. Other details, such as images, also help you understand the main idea.

 **Review the flyer. Then answer the questions that follow.**

**SAVE MONEY AND SUPPORT A CLEANER ENVIRONMENT**

**Join the Vanpool!**

See Philip for details about the new company vanpool.

6. What is the main idea of this flyer?

7. How does the image help you understand the main idea?

## Summarize the Main Idea

After previewing, identifying, reading, and looking for details, you are ready to summarize the main idea of a document.

 **Review the following guidelines. Then answer the questions.**

### The Best in Customer Service

1. Have a positive attitude when assisting customers.

2. Be knowledgeable and courteous.

3. Be visible and available to assist customers.

4. Go the extra mile to make customers happy.

8. What is the purpose of this document?

9. How would you summarize this document?

**GOT IT?** | **Use these strategies to determine the purpose and main idea of a workplace document:**

- Preview the text and identify the document's purpose.
- Read closely to determine the main idea.
- Look for images and other details that help clarify the main idea.
- Summarize the main idea and the most important details.

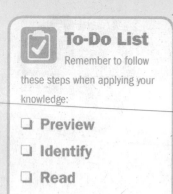

**To-Do List**

Remember to follow these steps when applying your knowledge:

☐ **Preview**

☐ **Identify**

☐ **Read**

☐ **Look**

☐ **Summarize**

# Apply Your Knowledge

Use the reading strategies you've learned to identify the purpose and main idea of workplace documents.

**Read each of the following scenarios and its accompanying document. Select the correct answer for each question.**

1. Owen works at a coffee shop. The shop's owner made the following checklist for Owen to use when he helps close for the night.

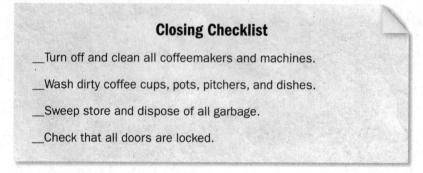

### Closing Checklist

__Turn off and clean all coffeemakers and machines.

__Wash dirty coffee cups, pots, pitchers, and dishes.

__Sweep store and dispose of all garbage.

__Check that all doors are locked.

**What are Owen's main responsibilities when closing the coffee shop?**

**A.** Making coffee for the following morning

**B.** Cleaning the shop and locking up

**C.** Ordering supplies for the shop

**D.** Taking inventory and setting the alarm

2. Alicia is training to work as a medical assistant. Before meeting with a patient for the first time, she receives the following e-mail from her trainer.

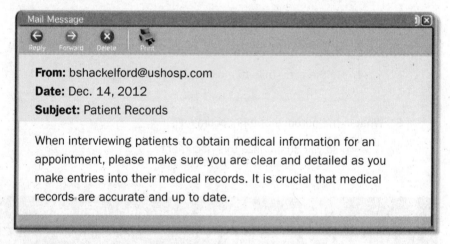

Mail Message

Reply    Forward    Delete    Print

**From:** bshackelford@ushosp.com
**Date:** Dec. 14, 2012
**Subject:** Patient Records

When interviewing patients to obtain medical information for an appointment, please make sure you are clear and detailed as you make entries into their medical records. It is crucial that medical records are accurate and up to date.

**What is the main purpose of this e-mail?**

**A.** To give instructions for recording patient information

**B.** To point out that patients often provide the wrong information

**C.** To explain where patients' medical records are located

**D.** To schedule an appointment to interview a new patient

**3.** David works for a computer company. He received the following order form, and he is responsible for getting the order ready for shipment.

| Item Number | Description | Quantity | Price (each) |
|---|---|---|---|
| 78735 | monitor | 1 | $150.00 |
| 79826 | keyboard | 1 | $50.00 |
| 84693 | mouse | 2 | $25.00 |
| 95038 | printer | 1 | $125.00 |
| | | Shipping (3-day) | $25.00 |
| | | Total | $400.00 |

**Based on the information in this order form, David should:**

**A.** Call the customer to find out if he or she wants to order paper.

**B.** Ask a co-worker to fill out the order form.

**C.** Contact the customer to find out if the order is complete.

**D.** Package the order quickly so it can ship within 3 days.

---

**In Real Life** | **Put Your Skills to Work!**

You work as a cook for a restaurant. Customers have recently complained that their dishes are over- or under-cooked. The head chef asks you to help him create documents that will help all of the cooks prepare certain dishes correctly.

 **Think about the problem you are facing and put your skills to work! What kind of documents should you create, and what information should you include? Explain your answers.**

**Workplace Tip**

When deciding what type of documents to create, think about:
- The purpose and main idea of each document
- What details you should include to make the main idea of the document clear

**Think About It!**

Which strategy will be most useful to you in the workplace, and why?

Using reading strategies will help you read and understand various documents in and out of the workplace. Some strategies will be more effective than others for certain types of documents. However, each is useful in helping you determine the purpose and main idea of a text.

**Answer Key**

**1.** B

**2.** A

**3.** D

# Test Your WRC Skills

**Understanding workplace documents requires a variety of reading skills. Read the scenarios and review each document. Select the answer you think best responds to the question.**

1. To help employees stay focused and to prevent computer viruses and malfunctioning, your company has distributed the following policy. What is the main idea of this document?

---

**Use of Company Computers**

The Company provides employees with computers to assist with job-related tasks. E-mail access and the Internet are available on all Company computers. However, these services are provided for work purposes only.

The Company reserves the right to monitor computer use. Employees using e-mail and Internet services for personal use may be subject to disciplinary action, up to and including termination.

---

A. ○  Employees may not access e-mail or the Internet on work computers.

B. ○  E-mail and Internet use are for work-related tasks only.

C. ○  Employees who access e-mail at work will be terminated.

D. ○  E-mail and Internet access has been disabled on work computers.

2. According to the order form, how many gallons of green paint did the customer order?

| Item Number | Item Description | Quantity | Price (each) |
|---|---|---|---|
| 78735 | white exterior primer (1 gallon) | 10 | $20.00 |
| 79826 | brown exterior stain (1 gallon) | 5 | $22.00 |
| 84693 | yellow exterior paint (1 gallon) | 12 | $25.00 |
| 95038 | green exterior paint (1 gallon) | 8 | $25.00 |
| | *Tax included on all purchases | | |

| | |
|---|---|
| Shipping | $45.00 |
| Total | $855.00 |

A. ○  12

B. ○  5

C. ○  8

D. ○  10

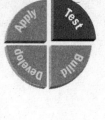

**3.** What is the purpose of the following memo?

> **To:** Crane Operators
> **From:** Management
> **Re:** Crane Inspection
>
> This memo is to inform you that all cranes will undergo a mandatory inspection on the morning of Thursday, November 29. As a result, crane operators scheduled to work Thursday are not required to arrive on site until 1:00 P.M.

| | | |
|---|---|---|
| **A.** | ◯ | To announce an inspection that will affect crane operators' schedules |
| **B.** | ◯ | To encourage crane operators to take Thursday off from work |
| **C.** | ◯ | To remind crane operators to inspect their cranes on Thursday |
| **D.** | ◯ | To announce that several cranes will need to be repaired |

**4.** Read this excerpt from your company's maternity leave policy. What is the main idea?

> When returning to work, the employee is entitled to the same or equivalent position with no loss of rights or privileges. Should the employee not return to work when released by her physician, she will be considered to have voluntarily terminated her employment.

| | | |
|---|---|---|
| **A.** | ◯ | Women must wait for their physician's recommendation before returning to work. |
| **B.** | ◯ | Women are entitled to return to their original job after pregnancy. |
| **C.** | ◯ | After pregnancy, women are encouraged to reapply for their old job. |
| **D.** | ◯ | Some women may decide to terminate their employment after pregnancy. |

**5.** You work in a manufacturing warehouse. According to this flyer, what should you do when you are done using tools and equipment?

> **Reminder**
>
> Please be sure to check out tools and equipment from the cage supervisor. Write your name neatly on the sign-out sheet. When you are through, check the equipment back in and cross your name off the sign-out sheet. Thank you.

| | | |
|---|---|---|
| **A.** | ◯ | Ask your supervisor to return the equipment to the cage. |
| **B.** | ◯ | Sign out the tools and equipment. |
| **C.** | ◯ | See if anybody else needs the equipment before checking it in. |
| **D.** | ◯ | Check in the equipment. |

**Check your answers on page 164.**

# Skills for the Workplace

## Identify the Source

Workplace documents come from many sources and are developed for different audiences. In a single day, you might receive an e-mail from your boss, read a set of guidelines from another department, and see a sign posted by Human Resources. Each of those documents was created by different people and was meant for a particular audience to read.

When reading a workplace material, it is important to identify where the material came from and for whom the material is intended.

- Knowing the author of a document can give you important insight into how to react to its contents. An e-mail from the company owner should be treated seriously, while an e-mail from a co-worker may not be as urgent.

- Knowing the audience can tell you whether the information applies to you. For example, a document about the appropriate dress code for work applies to all employees, not just you.

In many documents, the "From" and "To" lines identify the author and audience. For other documents, you may have to figure it out on your own.

## Workplace Scenario

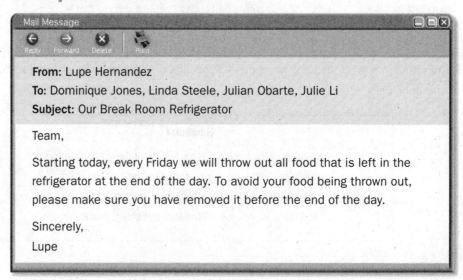

**From:** Lupe Hernandez
**To:** Dominique Jones, Linda Steele, Julian Obarte, Julie Li
**Subject:** Our Break Room Refrigerator

Team,

Starting today, every Friday we will throw out all food that is left in the refrigerator at the end of the day. To avoid your food being thrown out, please make sure you have removed it before the end of the day.

Sincerely,
Lupe

**1.** Lupe Hernandez is your boss. What does this tell you about the new rule regarding food left in the refrigerator? *The rule is official and is meant to be followed.*

# Workplace Practice

**You see the following sign posted in the main break room when you arrive to work on Monday:**

---

MANDATORY STAFF MEETING

9:00 A.M.

PLEASE MEET IN THE TRAINING ROOM.

---

1. Who is the sign from?

2. What does this tell you?

3. For whom is the sign intended?

*Company executives or the Human Resources department typically posts signs like this, which means the announcement is official and should be followed. The sign is probably intended for all workers because it is posted where everyone can see it.*

## Workplace Tip

Typically, any sign that is posted for all employees to see is an official notice that comes from the company's executive team.

## It's Your Turn!

1. On your first day at a new job, you receive a packet titled "Employee Manual." Who did the manual come from?

2. You receive an e-mail inviting you out to lunch with co-workers. Where can you look to see who sent it?

3. Which of the following is most likely to come from your boss: a company-wide memo about vacation days, an e-mail notifying you of an upcoming team meeting, or a poster about a city festival?

4. You receive the following memo:

   **To:** Jase Devon

   **From:** The Office of the President

   **Subject:** Early Closing

   **Date:** July 3, 2012

   In honor of the upcoming Independence Day celebrations, our offices will be closing at noon on Friday, July 3. Enjoy a safe 4th of July weekend.

   A. Who sent the memo?

   B. For whom was the memo intended?

5. Why is it important to identify the source of workplace information?

*It's Your Turn! Answer Key*
1. The Human Resources department
2. The "From" field
3. An e-mail notifying you of an upcoming team meeting
4A. The president of the company
4B. All company employees
5. Knowing whom a document comes from can help you identify how important or urgent it is.

# Chapter 1 Assessment

**Select the answer you think best responds to the question.**

**1.** What is the **MAIN** purpose of this document?

### DO YOUR PART!

We are trying to reduce energy costs in our building.
Please remember to:

· Turn off all lights in vacant conference rooms.

· Reuse scrap paper from containers in the copy room.

· Use energy-saving settings on your computers.

**Little changes can mean big energy savings!**

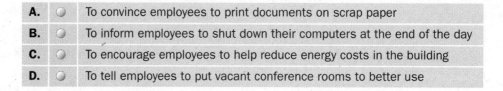

| | | |
|---|---|---|
| **A.** | ○ | To convince employees to print documents on scrap paper |
| **B.** | ○ | To inform employees to shut down their computers at the end of the day |
| **C.** | ○ | To encourage employees to help reduce energy costs in the building |
| **D.** | ○ | To tell employees to put vacant conference rooms to better use |

**2.** According to this procedure, what should lab employees do when the timer goes off?

**Lab Equipment Cleaning Procedure:**

1. Carefully wash your hands with warm water and soap.
2. Use the soap on the shelf above sink A to wash all equipment.
3. Put the equipment into one of the pans on the stove.
4. Fill the pan with water.
5. Put the lid on the pan.
6. Bring the water to a boil. Then set the timer for 15 minutes.
7. When the timer goes off, remove the pan from the stove.
8. Use the strainer to drain all excess water from the pan.
9. Let the equipment cool to room temperature.
10. Do not touch any equipment until it has cooled.

| | | |
|---|---|---|
| **A.** | ○ | Wash their hands with the soap above sink A. |
| **B.** | ○ | Remove the pan from the stove and drain the water. |
| **C.** | ○ | Fill the pan with water and then wash the equipment. |
| **D.** | ○ | Let the equipment cool to room temperature. |

**3.** According to this log, who returned laptop 2156-A on 2/19/2012?

**Laptop Sign-out Log**

| Employee Name | Date Borrowed | Laptop ID Number | Date Returned |
|---|---|---|---|
| J. Hernandez | 2/12/2012 | 2156-A | 2/14/2012 |
| O. Miller | 2/14/2012 | 2156-B | 2/15/2012 |
| A. Gilbert | 2/15/2012 | 2156-C | 2/19/2012 |
| R. Emery | 2/17/2012 | 2156-A | 2/19/2012 |

| | | |
|---|---|---|
| **A.** | ○ | J. Hernandez |
| **B.** | ○ | O. Miller |
| **C.** | ○ | A. Gilbert |
| **D.** | ○ | R. Emery |

**4.** What is the purpose of this memo?

**To:** All Cashiers

**From:** Ms. Akita

**RE:** Transfer Opportunities

We will be opening our downtown store in May. In addition, two new stores will be opening uptown in June. Cashiers who transfer to one of our new stores will be expected to help train the cashiers at our new locations. In return, they will receive a store-opening bonus. Employees interested in applying for a transfer should contact me for more information.

| | | |
|---|---|---|
| **A.** | ○ | To outline the policy for employees who would like to transfer |
| **B.** | ○ | To explain that the downtown store will be bigger than the uptown stores |
| **C.** | ○ | To explain the new schedule at the downtown store |
| **D.** | ○ | To encourage employees to work uptown |

**5.** According to this sign, which badge do you need to enter Work Site C?

**Work Site Admittance Rules**

**Clearance 1:** Green Badge
Work Site A Only

**Clearance 2:** Orange Badge
Work Site B Only

**Clearance 3:** Blue Badge
Work Sites B and D

**Clearance 4:** Yellow Badge
Work Sites A and C

| | | |
|---|---|---|
| **A.** | ○ | Green badge |
| **B.** | ○ | Blue badge |
| **C.** | ○ | Yellow badge |
| **D.** | ○ | Orange badge |

Check your answers on page 165.

 For more Chapter 1 assessment questions, please visit www.mysteckvaughn.com/WORK

# 2 Use Reading Strategies

Using pre-reading strategies and what you know about different types of texts can help you frame your purpose and comprehend what you read. In this chapter, you will practice previewing workplace documents and graphic displays, understanding sequence, making predictions, and identifying and understanding text features.

# Preview Workplace Documents

## Essential Tasks

**Preview material**
to anticipate content and organization

**Use text organization**
to locate information

## Build on What You Know

When you receive an e-mail, what is the first thing that you look for? Do you identify who the sender is? Perhaps you glance at the subject line to get a hint about what the e-mail is about. You usually do not begin reading an e-mail before you have some idea about what it will tell you. You **preview** the text to gather basic information before you read it in depth.

Knowing when and how to preview a text are very useful skills, especially in the workplace. For example, you may be asked to familiarize yourself with a large employee handbook on your first day of work. You can use previewing skills to decide which sections do not apply to you and which sections you should take time to read carefully. This lesson will teach you strategies to determine when and how to preview workplace documents.

### In Real Life | Kitchen Confusion

It is Emily's first day as a food preparer at the local pizza parlor. When she arrives, her supervisor asks her to review the basic food safety guidelines on the bulletin board in the kitchen. When Emily looks at the bulletin board, she finds several important-looking papers on it.

 **Discuss the following questions with a classmate.**

1. How might Emily find the document that she needs?

2. In what ways might the food safety guidelines look different from the other papers on the bulletin board?

3. What kind of information do you think will be on the document Emily is looking for?

**Teacher Reminder**
Review the teacher lesson at
www.mysteckvaughn.com/WORK

# Learning When to Preview

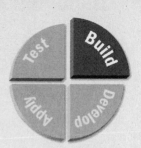

In Lessons 1 and 2, you learned that you preview a text to see what it is about. You can preview to find a text's main idea, to decide if a text will be useful to you, or to locate specific information within a text.

It is important to remember, however, that previewing is not a substitute for reading. Use previewing to help you:

- Understand at a glance what you will read, or
- Decide if you should read something in depth.

If you need to fully understand a document, you must read it completely and carefully.

 **Read the following scenarios. Decide if you can simply preview the text, or if you should read it in depth. Share your ideas with the class.**

4. You get a packet of information about health benefits at your workplace. You want to know if your dental checkup will be covered.

5. Your supervisor asks you to review and understand the cell phone policy located in the employee handbook.

6. You receive important instructions regarding the care of a dog being boarded at the veterinary clinic where you work.

7. You are asked to find a receipt filed in a binder with a variety of documents.

# Use What You Know

One strategy you can use to preview documents in the workplace is to use your background knowledge. You can use what you already know about certain types of documents and their formats to guess why they were written and for whom.

 **Discuss the following questions. Share your ideas with the class.**

8. Without reading the specifics of the agenda, what might happen at the beginning of the meeting? What might happen at the end?

9. Using what you know about agendas, what kinds of topics may be discussed?

10. What might be some purposes of this agenda?

> **Meeting Agenda**
>
> November 8, 2012
> Groups Attending:
> All Lead & Assistant Caregivers
>
> I. Roll Call
>
> II. Previous Meeting's Minutes
>
> III. Weekly Status Check-In
>    A. Morning Program
>    B. Afternoon Program
>
> IV. Upcoming Events
>
> V. Questions and Concerns

# Develop Your Skills

Using your background knowledge about text types and formats is just one strategy to help you preview a document. Below are some other ways to preview texts that you may encounter in the workplace.

## Skimming and Scanning

Skimming and scanning a document will help you gather useful information without having to read the entire text. When you skim and scan, look for titles, headings, subheads, bold or italicized words, pictures, and graphics to help you find what you need.

When you **skim** a text, you read it quickly to find the main idea. You might skim a text to:

- Understand the general meaning of a company memo.
- Determine if the information in an instruction manual will help you.

You **scan** a text to find specific information. You might scan a text to:

- Find the destination address on a shipping order.
- Identify the correct extension number from a list to transfer a call.

 **Read the following tasks. Place a check mark in the correct box.**

|  | Skim | Scan |
|---|---|---|
| **1.** Understand the main idea of a company's mission statement. |  |  |
| **2.** Look at a shift schedule to find what days you work. |  |  |
| **3.** Verify a client identification number on an order form. |  |  |
| **4.** Decide if a list of department policies applies to you. |  |  |

 **Skim and scan the following document. Discuss your answers to the questions with a classmate.**

> **NOTICE!**
>
> This office will be closed on January 1. All doors will be locked and no entry will be permitted. Before you leave on Friday, feel free to stop by the front desk to pick up a New Year's gift card, courtesy of the Human Resources department. We hope you enjoy your holiday weekend.

**5.** What is the main idea of this document?

**6.** When will the office be closed?

# TIPP?

Use the TIPP? strategy to help you remember what to look for when you preview a text.

| | |
|---|---|
| **T**itle | Look at the text's title, headings, and layout. |
| **I**ntroduction | Skim the introduction to get the main idea. |
| **P**aragraphs | Skim the first line of paragraphs and text boxes. |
| **P**ictures | Look at the graphics and illustrations. |
| **?** | Think of questions that you have about the text. |

**Look at the following document. Then complete the TIPP? chart below by explaining what each part tells you. Discuss the chart with a classmate.**

---

### HARASSMENT POLICY

Harassment of employees, supervisors, and third parties is strictly prohibited by law and will not be permitted.

Harassment consists of behavior that is deemed inappropriate, offensive, hostile, or disruptive to individuals in the workplace. Examples of such behavior include, but are not limited to, threats, sexual innuendo, physical assault, derogatory jokes or slurs, and vulgar posters or computer displays.

Report harassment to the Human Resources department at ext. 7653.

---

| | | |
|---|---|---|
| **7.** | **T**itle | |
| **8.** | **I**ntroduction | |
| **9.** | **P**aragraphs | |
| **10.** | **P**ictures | |
| **11.** | **?** | |

---

## GOT IT?

**Preview a text to find basic information before reading in depth. Preview with these strategies:**

- Use your background knowledge to identify a text type and form.
- Skim to find the main idea.
- Scan to locate specific information.
- Use TIPP? to determine what certain features are telling you about a text.

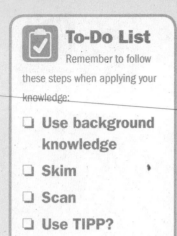
# Apply Your Knowledge

Previewing a text requires that you decide when previewing is appropriate and then use previewing strategies effectively.

**Read each of the following scenarios and preview the documents. Select the correct response for each question.**

1. Lin rides his bike to work every day and locks his bike on the rack in front of the building. One day he arrives and sees the following e-mail in his inbox.

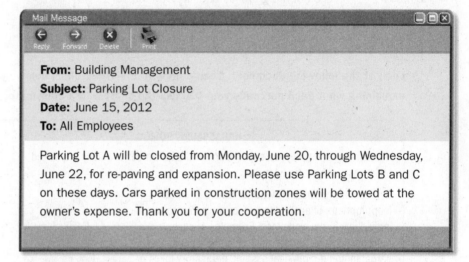

**From:** Building Management
**Subject:** Parking Lot Closure
**Date:** June 15, 2012
**To:** All Employees

Parking Lot A will be closed from Monday, June 20, through Wednesday, June 22, for re-paving and expansion. Please use Parking Lots B and C on these days. Cars parked in construction zones will be towed at the owner's expense. Thank you for your cooperation.

**Based on the subject of the e-mail, Lin will probably:**

**A.** Skim the e-mail to determine its main idea.

**B.** Scan the e-mail to find out when the parking lot will open.

**C.** Delete the e-mail because it does not apply to him.

**D.** Read the e-mail carefully so that he doesn't park in the wrong lot.

2. You have the flu and want to use a sick day. You have been with your company for seven months. You look up your company's sick day policy in the employee handbook.

**Sick Days**

**Eligibility:**
Employees are eligible to accrue sick days after six months of full-time employment.

**Policy:**
Once eligible, one paid sick day will be granted every two months for employees needing to take time off for illness or injury. Unused sick days will be forfeited at the end of the year. Sick days are not to be used as vacation days (see page 14) or personal days (see page 15). If an employee needs to take more time off, arrangements must be made with his or her supervisor.

**Where will you find information about whether or not you have qualified for sick days?**

A. On page 15

B. Under "Policy"

C. On page 14

D. Under "Eligibility"

3. You operate the ski lift at a mountain ski resort. Your supervisor asks you to review the following document with someone who is a new hire.

**Based on the title, what kind of information will you review?**

A. Your responsibilities

B. Company policies

C. New hire schedules

D. Safety warnings

> **Responsibilities of Ski Lift Operators**
>
> · Check that all passengers have a lift ticket
> · Help passengers exit and enter the lift safely
> · Maintain order among passengers in line

## In Real Life  Put Your Skills to Work!

You are working as an electrician's helper. The head electrician is having a difficult time repairing a client's television set. He can get the picture to appear, but the sound will not work. He asks you to look in his television repair instruction manual to locate some information that might help him find a solution.

 **Think about the problem you are facing and put your skills to work! How will you find the information you need? What skills can you use?**

**Workplace Tip**

When searching in the manual, would you think about:

• The purpose and format of an instruction manual?

• Scanning the table of contents to find a helpful chapter?

• Skimming a section to determine if it will be useful?

## Think About It!

**When can you simply preview a text, and when should you read it fully?**

Preview a text to find the main idea or some specific information, or to decide if the text will be helpful to you. Do not preview if you need to know and understand everything that a document says. Previewing strategies include using background knowledge, skimming, scanning, and TIPP? Some strategies work better than others for certain tasks.

**Answer Key**

1. C

2. D

3. A

# Test Your WRC Skills

**Previewing workplace documents is a useful skill that can be accomplished by applying several strategies. Read the following scenarios and review each document. Select the answer you think best responds to the question.**

1. Based on the subject line of this e-mail, what information can you expect to find?

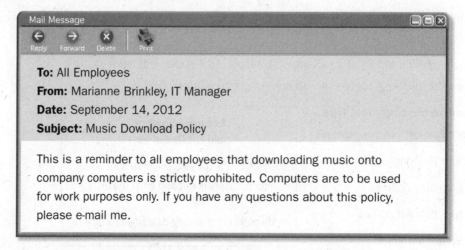

> **Mail Message**
>
> Reply   Forward   Delete   Print
>
> **To:** All Employees
> **From:** Marianne Brinkley, IT Manager
> **Date:** September 14, 2012
> **Subject:** Music Download Policy
>
> This is a reminder to all employees that downloading music onto company computers is strictly prohibited. Computers are to be used for work purposes only. If you have any questions about this policy, please e-mail me.

| A. | ○ | Information about how to download music |
| B. | ○ | Information about the IT manager |
| C. | ○ | Information about the music download policy |
| D. | ○ | Information about the various company computer policies |

2. What is the final step in naming a document?

**How to Name a Document**

1. Find the menu bar at the top of the screen.
2. Click FILE.
3. Click SAVE AS.
4. Type the name you have chosen for the file.
5. Select a location to save the document to.
6. Click SAVE.

| A. | ○ | Click FILE. |
| B. | ○ | Select a location to save the document to. |
| C. | ○ | Find the menu bar at the top of the screen. |
| D. | ○ | Click SAVE. |

**3.** Who is invited to the employee appreciation lunch?

> ### WE APPRECIATE YOU!
>
> Join us for the Smith and Company employee appreciation lunch, sponsored by the Human Resources department!
>
> **Who:** All temporary and permanent employees
> **When:** Friday, July 20
> **Where:** Clarence McDougal Dining Room
> **What:** Food, prizes, and fun!

| | | |
|---|---|---|
| **A.** | ○ | All temporary and permanent employees |
| **B.** | ○ | The Human Resources department |
| **C.** | ○ | Clarence McDougal |
| **D.** | ○ | Smith and Company |

**4.** Based on the title of this document, what information can you expect to find?

> ### NOTICE: ALTERNATE ROUTE DISTRIBUTION
>
> Due to flooding, Highway 39 is currently closed to vehicles. All drivers of bus routes with stops along the highway must report to their supervisors immediately to receive alternate routes.

| | | |
|---|---|---|
| **A.** | ○ | A reminder about when to take alternate routes |
| **B.** | ○ | A list of steps about how to take alternate routes |
| **C.** | ○ | An important note about receiving alternate routes |
| **D.** | ○ | A policy about when to take alternate routes |

**5.** Which training session is offered on May 22?

> ### TRAINING SESSION SCHEDULE
>
> **Non-Profit Campaigning Basics**
> Monday, May 21, 1:00–2:30
>
> **Making Your Pitch**
> Tuesday, May 22, 2:00–4:30
>
> **Practicing Your Skills**
> Wednesday, May 23, 1:30–3:00
>
> **Hitting the Streets**
> Thursday, May 24, 3:30–5:00

| | | |
|---|---|---|
| **A.** | ○ | Non-Profit Campaigning Basics |
| **B.** | ○ | Making Your Pitch |
| **C.** | ○ | Practicing Your Skills |
| **D.** | ○ | Hitting the Streets |

Check your answers on page 165.

# Preview Graphic Displays

## Essential Tasks

**Preview material** to anticipate content and organization

**Use text organization** to locate information

## Build on What You Know

Have you ever seen a preview poster for an upcoming movie and thought, "I can't wait to see that! I love action movies!" The bold, exciting title and image of a high-speed car chase tell you at a glance what the film will be about. They are clues that you can use to decide if the movie is something you will enjoy.

All documents have clues—movie posters, magazine articles, and even workplace documents. Reading the clues correctly can help you anticipate, or guess, what the text is about.

Many documents are made up of **graphic displays**, such as pictures, charts, or graphs. Each graphic display has its own set of clues that help you understand its meaning. This lesson will show you how to preview graphic displays that can be found in the workplace.

### In Real Life    What Do You Recommend?

Romero works as a concierge at an upscale hotel. Several guests approach his desk and ask him to recommend places to visit in the city. Romero takes out a map and scans it to locate some exciting city sites. He circles their locations for the guests. Then he uses a highlighter to show which roads to take to reach each destination.

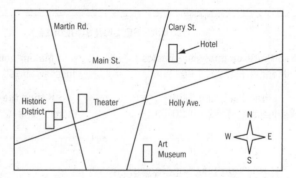

**Discuss the following questions with a classmate.**

1. Why do you think Romero used a map to help the hotel guests?

2. In what other ways could Romero give the hotel guests the information that they asked for?

3. Do you think the hotel guests will find the map useful? Why?

**Teacher Reminder**

Review the teacher lesson at www.mysteckvaughn.com/WORK

# What Is a Graphic Display?

Lesson 3 taught you how to preview workplace documents. Sometimes you will need to preview workplace documents that have graphic displays. Graphic displays use format, words, and images to provide information. They can include graphs, charts, tables, pictures, and maps. Here are some examples of types of graphic displays:

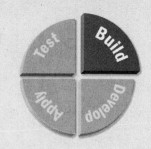

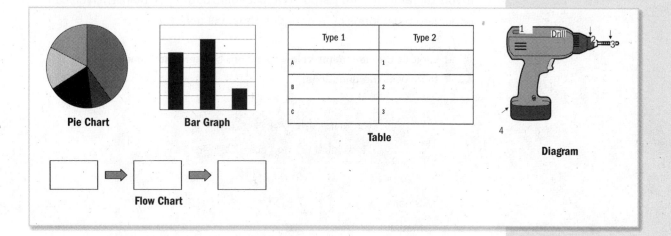

# When to Preview Graphic Displays

You should preview graphic displays for the same reasons you preview any other workplace document. Use previewing when you need to:

- Quickly understand the main idea of a graphic display, or
- Decide if you should read the graphic display in depth.

Don't forget that if you are required to know all of the material in a chart, graph, or other graphic display, you need to read it thoroughly.

> ## Workplace Tip
> A spreadsheet is one type of graphic display that you can create on a computer. It is usually used to organize large amounts of data.

 **Look at the line graph and read the scenarios. Decide if you can simply preview the graphic display or if you must read it in depth.**

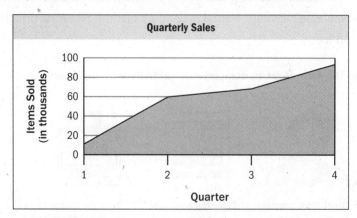

4. Your supervisor asks you if the graph will be useful for her presentation about items that the company sells.

5. You have been asked to transfer the data from the graph into a spreadsheet.

# Develop Your Skills

There are several strategies that you can use to preview graphic displays. You already know many of these strategies from Lesson 3.

## Use Background Knowledge

If you are familiar with purposes and layouts of graphic displays, you can anticipate what kinds of information they will give you.

 **Look at the document below. Use your background knowledge to answer the questions.**

| UNIFORM ORDER FORM | | |
|---|---|---|
| Individual uniform cost: $21.95 | | |
| Size | Quantity | Total |
| Small | 5 | $109.75 |
| Medium | 16 | $351.20 |
| Large | 12 | $263.40 |
| SHIPPING COST | | $10.00 |
| TOTAL COST | | $734.35 |

1. Order forms are usually what type of graphic display?

2. Think about what you already know about order forms. What information do you expect to find?

## Get a Clue!

Look for text features and visual clues to decide what a graphic display is about. Text features include titles, headings, subheads, bold or italicized words, labels, and captions. Visual clues may include pictures, directional arrows, and icons.

 **Use the flow chart to complete the activity with a partner.**

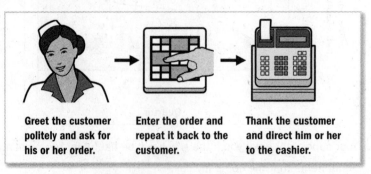

Greet the customer politely and ask for his or her order. → Enter the order and repeat it back to the customer. → Thank the customer and direct him or her to the cashier.

3. Identify the text features and visual clues in the flow chart. Discuss how they help you understand what the chart is about.

# Skimming and Scanning Graphic Displays

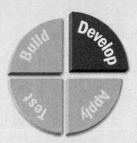

Skimming and scanning are especially useful when previewing complex graphic displays. Remember that when you skim, you read quickly to determine the main idea. You scan to locate specific information.

Look at the following **database**, which is a type of chart. It looks overwhelming. However, once you learn how to navigate the **rows** and **columns**, you will be able to find information that you are looking for. When you read a chart:

- Skim the column headings to see what kinds of information the chart contains.

- Use the column and row headings to scan for specific information. For example, imagine that you are asked to use the database below to confirm that Mr. Castillo received his order. First you would scan the "Name" column for Mr. Castillo's name. Then you would follow that row from left to right until you reach the "Delivered?" column.

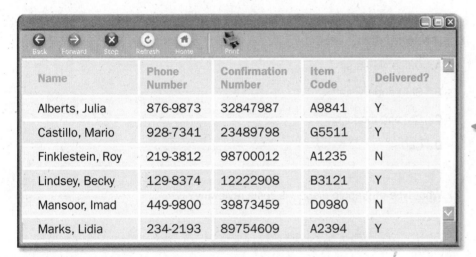

| Name | Phone Number | Confirmation Number | Item Code | Delivered? |
|------|--------------|---------------------|-----------|------------|
| Alberts, Julia | 876-9873 | 32847987 | A9841 | Y |
| Castillo, Mario | 928-7341 | 23489798 | G5511 | Y |
| Finklestein, Roy | 219-3812 | 98700012 | A1235 | N |
| Lindsey, Becky | 129-8374 | 12222908 | B3121 | Y |
| Mansoor, Imad | 449-9800 | 39873459 | D0980 | N |
| Marks, Lidia | 234-2193 | 89754609 | A2394 | Y |

**Use the database above to answer the following questions.**

4. Would this database be useful to determine how many customers have received their orders? How do you know?

5. Should you use this database to find the dates that customers received their orders? Why or why not?

## GOT IT?

**Use these strategies to preview graphic displays:**

- Use your background knowledge to anticipate content.

- Look for text features and visual clues.

- Skim to find the main idea.

- Scan to locate specific information.

## Workplace Tip

Look for patterns in the columns of databases. For example, the names might be listed in alphabetical order.

**Answer Key**

1. A chart or table

2. Types and quantities of items ordered, costs of items, and shipping costs

3. **Title**–Tells what the flow chart is about; **Labels**–Tell what to do in each step; **Pictures**–Show visually what to do in each step; **Directional arrows**–Show the order of the steps

4. Yes, you could count how many "Ys" and "Ns" are in the "Delivered?" column.

5. No, it only shows whether or not the orders were delivered.

**To-Do List**

Remember to follow these steps when applying your knowledge:

- ❏ **Use background knowledge**
- ❏ **Look for text features and visual clues**
- ❏ **Skim**
- ❏ **Scan**

# Apply Your Knowledge

Preview graphic displays to find out what they're about and to determine if they will be useful. Use the strategies you learned to preview effectively.

**Read each of the following scenarios and preview the graphic displays. Select the correct response for each question.**

1. Josie works in a toy-manufacturing factory. She is responsible for inspecting the packaging of action figures as they come through on a conveyer belt. In the middle of her shift, the conveyor belt makes a strange sound and suddenly stops. Josie needs to report that the machine is broken.

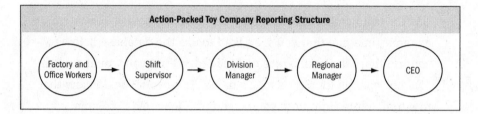

**Based on the information in the graphic display, Josie should report the problem to the:**

- **A.** Office workers
- **B.** Shift supervisor
- **C.** Division manager
- **D.** CEO

2. What type of graphic display is Josie reviewing?

3. You have just received your paycheck in the mail. When you open it, you find that the net pay is much less than you expected. You want to make sure that your hourly rate is listed correctly at $9 an hour.

| Payroll Stub | | | | |
|---|---|---|---|---|
| Earnings | Rate | Hours | This Period | Year-to-Date |
| **Regular** | $7.00 | 40 | $280.00 | $1,120.00 |
| Gross Pay | | | $280.00 | $1,120.00 |
| **Deductions** | | | | |
| Federal Tax | | | $42.00 | $168.00 |
| Social Security | | | $11.00 | $44.00 |
| Medicare | | | $8.00 | $32.00 |
| State Tax | | | $31.00 | $124.00 |
| Misc. | | | 0 | |
| **Total** | | | $92.00 | $368.00 |
| **Net Pay** | | | $188.00 | $752.00 |

**Based on the payroll stub, your hourly rate is listed as:**

**A.** $8.00

**B.** $40.00

**C.** $7.00

**D.** $280.00

4. Would the graphic display in #3 be useful in determining how much you can expect your pay to increase in the next year? Why or why not?

## In Real Life   Put Your Skills to Work!

Last Friday your supervisor asked you to submit the shifts you are available to work next week. She collected each employee's requests and has asked you to put the information into a schedule that can be posted in the office.

 **Think about the problem you are facing and put your skills to work! What kind of graphic display will you use to create the schedule? Explain your reasons.**

## Think About It!

**Which types of graphic displays do you find easy to read? Which do you find challenging?**

**How will you improve your ability to understand graphic displays in the workplace?**

Graphic displays come in many shapes and sizes. Some are quite simple, while others can appear very complex. If you are familiar with the purposes and general organization of graphic displays, you can understand even the most intimidating or complex documents. Use the strategies you learned to help you preview the graphic displays you encounter. Remember to draw on your background knowledge, look for text features and visual clues, skim for the main idea, and scan to locate specific information.

**Answer Key**

**1.** B

**2.** Flow chart or organizational chart

**3.** C

**4.** No, the purpose of a payroll stub is to show how much money you are currently paid, not how much you will be paid in the future.

# Test Your WRC Skills

**Preview graphic displays with a variety of strategies. Read the following questions and review each graphic display. Select the answer you think best responds to the question.**

**1.** What is the code number for pears?

| Item | Code # |
|------|--------|
| Apple | 3014 |
| Banana | 3027 |
| Peach | 3078 |
| Pear | 3066 |
| Tangerine | 3098 |

A. ○ 3078

B. ○ 3014

C. ○ 3098

D. ○ 3066

**2.** What type of product makes up the largest amount of this store's inventory?

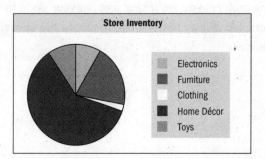

Store Inventory

Electronics
Furniture
Clothing
Home Décor
Toys

A. ○ Electronics

B. ○ Furniture

C. ○ Clothing

D. ○ Home décor

**3.** What information can you expect to find in this diagram?

**FORKLIFT**
Overhead guard
Mast
Counterweight
Load apron
forks

A. ○ Parts of a forklift

B. ○ How to use a forklift

C. ○ Different types of forklifts

D. ○ When to use a forklift

**4.** When does the customer service department at Handy's Hardware receive the most calls?

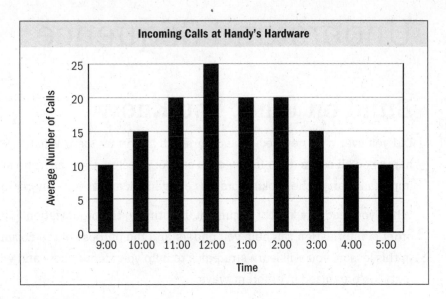

Incoming Calls at Handy's Hardware

| A. | ○ | 9:00 |
|----|----|------|
| B. | ○ | 11:00 |
| C. | ○ | 12:00 |
| D. | ○ | 5:00 |

**5.** Based on the title of this flow chart, what information can you expect to find?

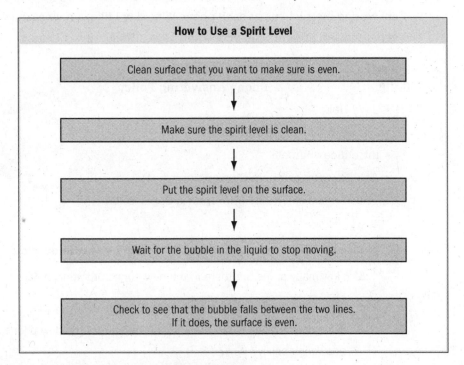

How to Use a Spirit Level

Clean surface that you want to make sure is even.

↓

Make sure the spirit level is clean.

↓

Put the spirit level on the surface.

↓

Wait for the bubble in the liquid to stop moving.

↓

Check to see that the bubble falls between the two lines.
If it does, the surface is even.

| A. | ○ | Instructions for ordering a spirit level |
|----|----|------|
| B. | ○ | Instructions for making a spirit level |
| C. | ○ | Instructions for using a spirit level |
| D. | ○ | Instructions for cleaning a spirit level |

Check your
answers on
page 166.

# Understand Sequence

## Build on What You Know

Did you ever try a new recipe and forget an important step? What happened? If cooks don't follow each step of a recipe, they may skip an important part of the cooking process or overlook an essential ingredient.

When you read any kind of document, identifying the organization and order of information can help you understand the purpose of the document. In this lesson, you will learn strategies to help you identify how and why texts are organized in different ways.

---

### In Real Life  Phone Folly

In an effort to improve customer service, Manuel, the manager of an auto repair shop, is implementing a new phone answering policy. Manuel trains all of his employees and posts the following phone answering instructions at each phone. One day Luke, a new cashier, is very busy. He answers the phone and says, "Hello, this is Luke."

**Phone Answering Policy**

- Say "Hello."
- Thank the customer for calling.
- Introduce yourself.
- Ask how you can help the customer.
- Transfer the call to the appropriate department.

**Discuss the following questions. Share your ideas with the class.**

1. How many steps are there in the new phone answering policy?

2. Did Luke forget any steps?

3. What do you think is the most important step of the new phone answering policy? Why?

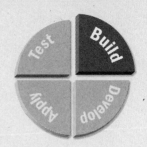

# Text Organization

In previous lessons, you learned about various types of workplace documents such as order forms, instructions, schedules, and agendas. Each of these documents is organized in a different way, but all of them have some kind of order, or **sequence**. Some documents may be organized using beginning, middle, and ending paragraphs. Other documents may use numbers and graphics to organize information.

 **Look at the documents below. With a classmate, compare how each document is organized.**

| Meeting Agenda |
|---|
| January 12, 2012 |
| I. Introductions |
| II. New Procedures |
| III. Closing Thoughts |

| Work Schedule | | | | |
|---|---|---|---|---|
| M | T | W | Th | F |
| 8:00–5:00 | 9:00–6:00 | 10:00–7:00 | 8:00–5:00 | 8:00–5:00 |

Understanding the organization of a document can help you follow procedures or processes throughout your workday. In some offices, there are **troubleshooting** documents that can help you follow a procedure to assess or solve a problem. The following flow chart helps workers follow a procedure when they have a computer problem:

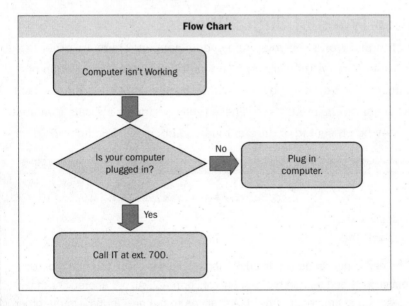

Flow Chart

> **Workplace Tip**
>
> To understand how a workplace document is organized, look for:
> - Paragraph organization
> - Numbers
> - Graphics

 **Look at the flow chart and think about its organization. Then read and answer the questions.**

4. How is the flow chart organized?

5. Do the graphics help you understand the chart?

6. Where would this chart be posted?

7. Is this type of chart easy to understand? Why or why not?

# Develop Your Skills

Remember, to understand workplace documents, you can scan them for important clues about their organization. These clues may be obvious from a document's graphics or its layout. Other documents may use certain words and phrases that will help you follow the document's sequence.

## Scanning for Signal Words

An important strategy to use when you look at a document is to scan for key words called **signal words**. The list below has common signal words that will help you understand the sequence of many workplace documents.

| | | | | |
|---|---|---|---|---|
| first | second | third | then | next |
| finally | before | after | later | last |

 **Discuss your daily work schedule with a classmate or friend. Then look at the clocks below.**

1. Use signal words from the list above to explain what you do at the time indicated on each clock.

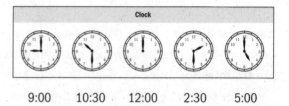

Clock

9:00    10:30    12:00    2:30    5:00

## Other Types of Signal Words

Not all signal words tell you when events happen. There are other key words and phrases that can help you understand the organization of a document. For example, you may come across words and phrases such as *however* or *on the other hand*. These types of signals indicate that a new idea may be presented or different viewpoints may be compared.

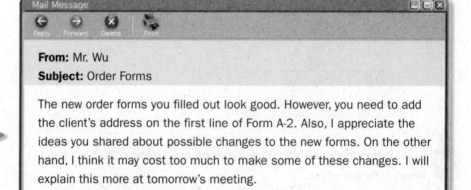

Mail Message

Reply    Forward    Delete    Print

**From:** Mr. Wu
**Subject:** Order Forms

The new order forms you filled out look good. However, you need to add the client's address on the first line of Form A-2. Also, I appreciate the ideas you shared about possible changes to the new forms. On the other hand, I think it may cost too much to make some of these changes. I will explain this more at tomorrow's meeting.

> ### Workplace Tip
> When you read workplace documents, look for signal words to understand their organization and purpose.

**Read the e-mail below.**

2. Identify the words or phrases in the e-mail that are important signal words.

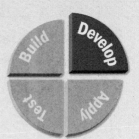

# Scanning for Context Clues

In addition to signal words, there are other hints that can help you understand workplace documents. Some documents are organized in a clear order but may contain unfamiliar or difficult words. When you encounter a word you don't know, you can use the context, or overall meaning, of a document to help figure out the word's meaning.

**Context clues** include:

- Words that come before or after the unfamiliar word
- Graphics or icons surrounding the word
- Overall meaning of the document

 **Use the information in the notice below to complete each item.**

---

**Work areas are QUIET areas.**

· Please keep your voice down.
· Use headphones when using any audio.
· Keep your cell phone ringers off.

This keeps our office quiet and **tranquil** so people can concentrate.

---

3. Explain how each of the following context clues can help you understand the meaning of the word *tranquil*.

- Graphics: _____

- Words: _____

- Overall meaning: _____

4. Based on the information in the notice, write your own definition for the word *tranquil*.

5. Did you notice any other clues you could use to help you understand the meaning of *tranquil*?

---

**GOT IT?** | **Identifying sequence and using context clues can help you understand workplace documents. Remember to:**

- Scan a document's layout to find clues about its organization.
- Identify signal words to determine the order of instructions.
- Look for context clues around a difficult word to figure out its meaning.

# Apply Your Knowledge

Identifying signal words and context clues are key steps to understanding workplace documents.

**Read each of the following scenarios. Then select the correct response for each question.**

1. At the beginning of each workday, Elena stops at her manager's office and signs her time sheet. Today Elena's manager tells her that the company now requires employees to use the new online time sheet system.

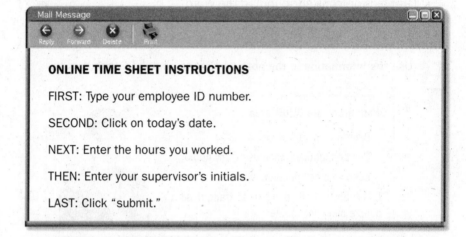

**Mail Message**
Reply   Forward   Delete   Print

**ONLINE TIME SHEET INSTRUCTIONS**

FIRST: Type your employee ID number.

SECOND: Click on today's date.

NEXT: Enter the hours you worked.

THEN: Enter your supervisor's initials.

LAST: Click "submit."

**Before Elena clicks on the date, she must:**

**A.** Enter her supervisor's initials.

**B.** Type her employee ID number.

**C.** Click "submit."

**D.** Enter the hours she worked.

2. What might happen if Elena skips a step of the instructions?

3. On your lunch break, you see this flyer posted in the break room:

> **NEW GET FIT PROGRAM!**
>
> **Our company now offers these valuable incentives for healthy employees:**
>
> · Free pedometer
> · Gym membership rebates
> · Free consultations with a nutritionist

**Based on the information in the flyer, an incentive is something that:**

**A.** Makes people healthier

**B.** Saves time and energy

**C.** Encourages people to take action

**D.** Keeps track of time

---

**In Real Life** | **Put Your Skills to Work!**

You work at a construction site. One morning, as you walk past a coworker's workstation, you trip over the cord to a power saw. The saw falls to the ground and breaks. When you tell your boss, he realizes that the group needs formal safety procedures to prevent accidents from happening. The procedures should be something that workers can follow at the end of each day to make sure all work areas are clean and safe. He asks you to help develop the procedures.

 **Think about the problem you are facing and put your skills to work! What kind of steps would you include in the safety procedures? What order would you put them in?**

> **Workplace Tip**
>
> When creating your safety procedures, did you think about:
> - The importance of the sequence of steps?
> - Using signal words?
> - Including context that will help all workers understand the procedures?

## Think About It!

**What type of text organization do you find easiest to understand? Why?**

**If you are reading workplace documents and don't understand a word or phrase, what can you do?**

Think about context and identify sequence to help you understand the purpose and to follow the procedure of all kinds of workplace documents. Look for important signal words and context clues when you are reading a document. This will help you understand the document's sequence and determine the meaning of words you may not know.

**Answer Key**

**1.** B

**2.** Answers will vary.

**3.** C

# Test Your WRC Skills

**Understanding the sequence of workplace documents requires that you be aware of signal words and text organization. Read the following scenarios and review each document. Select the answer you think best responds to the question.**

**1.** What is the second step of the night crew's cleaning instructions?

---

**Night Crew Cleaning Instructions:**

Please sweep under all desks. Then mop the floor. Empty the mop water into the proper drain. Put away the broom, mop, and any buckets you used.

---

| | | |
|---|---|---|
| **A.** | ○ | Empty the mop water. |
| **B.** | ○ | Sweep the floor. |
| **C.** | ○ | Put away the broom. |
| **D.** | ○ | Mop the floor. |

**2.** In the context of this memo, what does the word ***punctual*** mean?

---

**MEMO**

**From:** Department Supervisors
**To:** All Employees
**Subject:** Lateness Policy

It is important that you are on time every day. You are expected to be at your desk at the time designated by your supervisor. If you are not ***punctual*** on a regular basis, you will receive a letter in your personnel file.

---

| | | |
|---|---|---|
| **A.** | ○ | Cleaning your desk |
| **B.** | ○ | Being on time |
| **C.** | ○ | Receiving a letter |
| **D.** | ○ | Reading a personnel file |

3. In the instructions below, which step comes directly **BEFORE** asking if the patient is a new or existing patient?

---

**Reception Desk Instructions**

1. Have the patient sign in.
2. Scan the patient's insurance card.
3. Ask if the patient is a new or existing patient.
4. If the patient is new, hand him or her form #107.
5. If the patient is an existing patient, hand him or her form #108.

---

| | | |
|---|---|---|
| **A.** | ○ | Having the patient sign in |
| **B.** | ○ | Scanning the patient's insurance card |
| **C.** | ○ | Handing the patient form #107 |
| **D.** | ○ | Handing the patient form #108 |

4. In this note, what does the word *collaborate* mean?

---

Tom,

We are running out of time on this project. I would like you and Luis to team up and *collaborate* to complete all order forms, invoices, and client notices.

---

| | | |
|---|---|---|
| **A.** | ○ | Work together |
| **B.** | ○ | Write an order form |
| **C.** | ○ | Talk to clients |
| **D.** | ○ | Run out of time |

5. What step comes **AFTER** your supervisor signs your request?

---

REMINDER TO ALL EMPLOYEES: To apply for overtime hours, you must get an Overtime Request Form from the Payroll department. Then fill out the first three sections of the form and have your supervisor sign it. Return your signed request form to the Payroll department.

---

| | | |
|---|---|---|
| **A.** | ○ | Getting the form from the Payroll department |
| **B.** | ○ | Filling out the first three sections of the request form |
| **C.** | ○ | Returning the signed request form to the Payroll department |
| **D.** | ○ | Asking your supervisor for permission to work overtime |

Check your answers on page 166.

# Make Predictions

## Essential Tasks

**Use text format and features** to find specific information

**Recognize signal words** that help organize text

## Build on What You Know

At the beginning of most books, you will find a table of contents. Look back to the Table of Contents of this book. What are the first things you notice about these pages? How are they organized?

A table of contents helps you **predict** what a book will be about. Similarly, the chapter headings listed in the Table of Contents help you predict what information you will read in each chapter. When you want to find information in this book, you can scan the headings in the Table of Contents to find the chapter you want and its page numbers.

This lesson will teach you how to use text features to make predictions about the content of workplace documents. This strategy will help you understand the sequence, organization, and meaning of many documents.

### In Real Life  Urgent E-Mails

Pablo arrives at work and finds a note from his boss, Ms. Park. In the note, Ms. Park asks Pablo to print the urgent e-mails she sent him yesterday and bring ten copies to the morning staff meeting.

When he clicks on his inbox, Pablo sees 17 messages with yesterday's date, and he does not have time to open and read each e-mail. He knows that Ms. Park often uses different subject labels when she sends urgent messages. As he is scrolling through the most recent messages in his inbox list, Pablo sees the following:

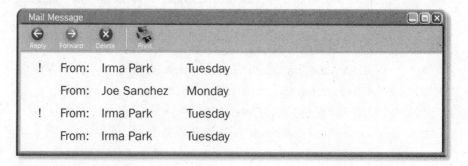

**Discuss the following questions. Share your ideas with the class.**

**1.** What do you notice about the e-mails from Ms. Park?

**2.** Why do you think some of the e-mails have exclamation points?

**Teacher Reminder**
Review the teacher lesson at
www.mysteckvaughn.com/WORK

## Using Text Features to Make Predictions

In Lessons 3 and 4, you learned about skimming and scanning different types of documents to locate information. You used your previewing skills to understand how text is organized in various documents, including charts and graphs. The layout of each of these workplace documents gives you hints about what it will be about. When you scan the layout of documents, remember to look for:

- Headings and subheadings
- Photographs and illustrations
- Captions
- Signal words and phrases
- Words in bold print or italics

As you read, keeping these organizational features in mind will help you predict what information you might find in a document. Predicting can help you focus on a document's content and understand its overall purpose.

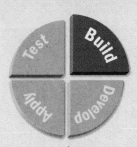

> **Workplace Tip**
>
> Many workplace documents have special features that help you:
> - Understand their purpose
> - Predict what they are about

 **Every month, SRM Industries sends out a newsletter to keep their employees informed about company news. Read the table of contents from the June edition. Then discuss the questions with a classmate.**

---

## SRM Newsletter *June Edition*

- **Congratulations, Matt, Employee of the Month!** – full story, page 1

- **New Branch Opening Next Week** – page 2

- *Important:* **Changes to Overtime Policies** – page 4

- **Interview with Our Company Director** – page 6

- **Pictures from the Pot Luck Luncheon** – page 8

- **June Birthdays** – page 10

---

3. What types of headings do you see on the newsletter cover page?

4. What information do you think you would find on page 5?

5. Which article should everyone in the company read?

# Develop Your Skills

The purpose of a document, its graphics, and its signal words and phrases are all valuable clues that can help you predict the document's content.

## Predicting Content in Workplace Documents

Sometimes you may only need to see an important word or phrase to make predictions about a document. You may only see a book's title and be able to predict what the book is about. Making this type of broad prediction about what you expect to find in a book can help you identify the right place to look for specific information.

### Workplace Tip

When you need to find information in a workplace manual, look at the manual's title and the images on the cover for hints about its content.

 **Look at the three manuals below and answer the questions.**

Employee Handbook

Safety in the Workplace

Company Directory

1. Using each manual's title to predict, what might you find in each manual?

2. Which manual would help you find information about your company's dress code?

Sometimes you will need to use more than just a title to make predictions. When you need to understand specific information in a chart, reading the title alone may not give you enough information to make predictions.

 **Look at the rows and columns of the sign-up sheet below.**

| Company Picnic Sign-up Sheet | |
| --- | --- |
| **Food/Drinks Needed** | **Name** |
| Lemonade | Michael |
| Hamburgers | Joe |
| Hot Dogs | Joe |
| Fruit | Angela |
| Salad | Andy |
| Ketchup/Mustard | Sylvia |

3. Which text features help you find information in the chart?

4. What did Andy sign up to bring?

# Using Prior Knowledge to Make Predictions

In addition to using text features, you can use what you already know to make predictions. Connecting what you know with what you think may happen will help you understand what you read.

You already know that signal words and phrases help you understand important workplace instructions. You also know that identifying the sequence, or order, of workplace documents can help you understand their purpose. These things can also help you make predictions about what you will read in a document and how you should use the information.

 **Read the evacuation procedure from a day care center and answer the questions that follow. Discuss your answers with a classmate.**

### EVACUATION PROCEDURE

1. WALK, DON'T RUN!!

2. Escort all children to the nearest exit.

3. Proceed to your department's designated meeting place.

4. Staff members: take roll and account for each child.

5. ONLY directors will administer first aid, as needed.

6. If necessary, begin phoning children's emergency contacts.

**5.** How is the evacuation procedure organized?

**6.** What do you notice about the first step of the instructions?

**7.** What can you predict about the step that might come after step 6?

**8.** Where should this type of document be posted?

---

**GOT IT?** Making predictions can help you understand workplace documents. To make predictions:

- Utilize titles, headings, and other text features.

- Make connections to what you already know.

- Think about what you expect the document to be about.

- Think about what may come next in processes and procedures.

# Apply Your Knowledge

Making predictions requires that you scan documents for important text features and signal words.

**Read each of the scenarios and select the correct response for each question.**

1. You just learned that a safety inspection is planned for your building. You have two days to prepare for this inspection. You get out your safety manual to find more information and open it to this page:

**TABLE OF CONTENTS**

**Chapter 1**
Introduction...........................................1–6
Safety Overview....................................7–14
Proper Safety Equipment......................15–19
Employee Safety Training......................20–29

**Chapter 2**
Safety Inspections...............................30–39
First-Aid Procedures.............................40–50

**What pages cover safety inspections?**

A. 1–6

B. 15–19

C. 30–39

D. 40–50

2. After working as a part-time employee for a year, you have been hired for a full-time position. As a full-time employee, you are eligible for health benefits. You go to the Human Resources office to apply for benefits and see this poster:

The following health benefits are offered to full-time employees:

• Medical    • Dental    • Vision

**\*YOU MUST ATTEND THE ENROLLMENT MEETING ON <u>NOVEMBER 1st</u> TO APPLY FOR BENEFITS\***

*For more information, see Cindy in Human Resources.*

**Based on the organization of the poster, the most important information is:**

**A.** The company's dental coverage

**B.** The date of the enrollment meeting

**C.** The name of the person in Human Resources

**D.** The company's vision plan

**3.** What special text features are used in the poster?

**4.** Do you think these text features help you understand the content of the poster? Why or why not?

## In Real Life — Put Your Skills to Work!

Your department has doubled in size over the last year. Your supervisor decides that a department handbook needs to be created so that all employees are aware of departmental information. Your supervisor asks you to create a Table of Contents for the handbook.

 **Think about the problem you are facing and put your skills to work! What departmental information should be included in the handbook? What order should the information be presented in? How can you set up the Table of Contents to help readers be able to predict where to find certain information? Explain your ideas.**

> **Workplace Tip**
>
> When creating your Table of Contents, did you think about:
> * What text features to use?
> * What signal words to use?
> * What order to present the information in?

## Think About It!

*How can text features and signal words help you make predictions about the content of a workplace document?*

Identifying special text features and signal words can help you predict what a document might be about and understand its overall organization and purpose. Making predictions about a document can help you find and understand the information you need.

**Answer Key**

**1.** C

**2.** B

**3.** Bulleted list, bold print, italics, asterisks

**4.** Answers will vary.

# Test Your WRC Skills

**Making predictions about the content of workplace documents requires that you use a variety of text features and signal words. Read the following scenarios and review each document. Select the answer you think best responds to the question.**

**1.** According to this sign, what step do employees complete **AFTER** they prepare a sandwich?

> **Sandwich Makers:**
>
> 1. Wash hands thoroughly.
> 2. Put on plastic gloves.
> 3. Prepare a sandwich for the customer.
> 4. Give the sandwich to a cashier.

| | | |
|---|---|---|
| **A.** | ○ | Wash hands thoroughly. |
| **B.** | ○ | Put on plastic gloves. |
| **C.** | ○ | Give the sandwich to a cashier. |
| **D.** | ○ | Give the sandwich to the customer. |

**2.** In this return procedure, what should employees do **LAST**?

> **Handling Returns**
>
> **First,** greet the customer. **Second,** ask for the customer's receipt. **Third,** match the code on the item's label with the item code on the receipt. **Next,** scan the bar code on the receipt and circle the item being returned. **Then** return the receipt to the customer. **Finally,** thank the customer for shopping at the store!

| | | |
|---|---|---|
| **A.** | ○ | Ask for the customer's receipt. |
| **B.** | ○ | Thank the customer for shopping at the store. |
| **C.** | ○ | Scan the bar code on the receipt. |
| **D.** | ○ | Circle the item being returned. |

**3.** Who cleaned the fitting room at ten o'clock on Monday?

### Fitting Room Checklist

| TIME | Monday | Tuesday | Wednesday | Thursday | Friday |
|------|--------|---------|-----------|----------|--------|
| 9:00 | T.L. | S.B. | T.L. | T.L. | T.L. |
| 10:00 | S.B. | K.P. | S.B. | S.B. | S.B. |
| 11:00 | H.M. | H. M. | T.L. | T.L. | T.L. |
| 12:00 | J.T. | P.W. | S.B. | S.B. | S.B. |

A. ○ T.L.
B. ○ S.B.
C. ○ K.P.
D. ○ J.T.

**4.** You are a new employee in Group B. On which day will you have computer training?

### New Employee Trainings

| · Safety Training | · Computer Training |
|---|---|
| Group A: March 3rd | Group A: March 10th |
| Group B: March 4th | Group B: March 11th |

A. ○ March 3rd
B. ○ March 4th
C. ○ March 10th
D. ○ March 11th

**5.** Machine Services, Inc., has jobs in which of the following locations?

| | | |
|---|---|---|
| **A-1 Lumber Company** | Headquarters: Austin, TX | Jobs in: Dallas, TX  Brooklyn, NY |
| **Thompson & Sons Furniture** | Headquarters: Springfield, MA | Jobs in: Boston, MA  San Diego, CA |
| **Machine Services, Inc.** | Headquarters: Norman, OK | Jobs in: Norman, OK  Forth Worth, TX |

A. ○ Fort Worth, TX
B. ○ Brooklyn, NY
C. ○ Boston, MA
D. ○ Dallas, TX

Check your
answers on
page 167.

# Skills for the Workplace

## Identify Text Features

As you have learned, workplace documents can include many different features, such as titles, headings, bold print, italics, charts, and lists. These **text features**:

- *Organize* the text in a logical way,
- Present information *quickly*,
- Make the text more *understandable*, and
- Show which parts are most *important*.

Use the chart below to find out more about each text feature:

| Text Feature | Example | Why It Is Used |
| --- | --- | --- |
| **Chart** | You're looking at one! | In a chart, information is organized into vertical columns and horizontal rows. Information can be found quickly by using the column headings at the top and the row headings on the left. |
| **Title** | WorkSkills™ Reading | A title tells what the document is about. It can help you decide how carefully you should read a document or if you need to read it at all. |
| **Headings** | **Identify Text Features** (see above) | A heading tells what a part of a document is about. Headings can help you locate information more easily. |
| **Bold Print** | **bold** | Bold print helps important information stand out. In this book, a bold word let's you know you can find its meaning in the Glossary. |
| **Italics** | *italics* | Like bold print, italics are another way of making important information stand out. |
| **Bulleted List** | • Item<br>• Item<br>• Item | A bulleted list presents related information in a short, easy-to-read way. |
| **Numbered List** | 1. Item<br>2. Item<br>3. Item | Numbered lists are used when the order of the items is important, such as steps in a safety procedure. |

## Workplace Scenario

- Look at the first paragraph on this page again. Which text features do you notice? *Bold print, a bulleted list, italics*

- What do the text features tell about the information in a paragraph? *Bold print:* text features *is a term from the Glossary; bulleted list: the items in the list are all related to text features; italics:* organize, quickly, understandable, *and* important *are especially important words*

# Workplace Practice

You work as a medical assistant and receive this flyer with your paycheck:

**To:** All Medical Assistants

**From:** Medical Errors Task Force

**Subject:** New Patient Bar Coding System

As part of our ongoing effort to reduce medical errors, we will be implementing a new patient bar coding system. The new system will go into effect at the beginning of next month. **Attendance at one of the training sessions below is mandatory.**

- Tuesday, June 21, at 9:00 A.M.
- Wednesday, June 29, at 3:00 P.M.
- Thursday, June 30, at 7:00 P.M.

*Please notify your supervisor and Kervin Johnston (extension 3508) about which training session you will attend.*

**Workplace Tip**

It is a good idea to read any information that comes with your paycheck very carefully. Many official notices are distributed this way.

- Which text features do you notice in this flyer? *Headings, bold print, bulleted list, italics*

- What do these text features tell you? *Headings: who the flyer is for, who it is from, what it is about; bold print: mandatory attendance is important; bulleted list: all training sessions are probably the same; italics: it is important to notify your supervisor and Kervin Johnston*

- How important do you think the new patient bar coding system is to this clinic? How important is the goal of reducing medical errors? *Both are very important to the clinic.*

## It's Your Turn!

1. You receive a handout titled "Urgent Computer Security Updates." Should you read it right away or set it aside for later?

2. The same handout includes a numbered list of steps. After reading the document, which step should you complete first?

3. You work at a call center and see a chart with employees' names listed on the left side and the following column headings across the top: "Calls taken," "Average call duration," and "Caller satisfaction." How would you find out how satisfied callers have been with your service?

4. Why do you think the call center posted this chart?

5. Your boss gives you a document with one section highlighted. The heading of the highlighted section is "Essential Work Station Tools." Under the heading is a bulleted list. What should you do after receiving this document?

*It's Your Turn!* **Answer Key**

**1.** Read it right away.

**2.** Step number 1

**3.** Look for the row heading with your name; then go across that row until you get to the "Caller satisfaction" column.

**4.** So employees can know their performance in these areas

**5.** Check your work station to make sure you have all of the tools listed in the bulleted list.

# Chapter 2 Assessment

**Select the answer you think best responds to the question.**

**1.** In the document below, what does the word *submit* mean?

> **To:** All Employees
> **From:** Human Resources
> **Re:** Time sheets
>
> The office will be closed Friday, July 4. Please **submit** your time sheet to your supervisor by noon on Thursday, July 3, so that your hours will be processed in time for the upcoming pay period.

A. ○ Type
B. ○ Throw away
C. ○ Turn in
D. ○ Print out

**2.** Based on the title of this document, what information can you expect to find?

> **New Building Security Measures**
>
> 1. Employees must wear their photo ID badges at all times.
> 2. Guests must sign in and wear a temporary badge at all times.
> 3. Employees will need to use swipe cards to enter side entrances.

A. ○ New measures regarding building security
B. ○ New measures regarding payroll
C. ○ New measures regarding vacation time
D. ○ New measures regarding parking passes

**3.** How many total hours did Jan work?

| Time Sheet | | Employee: Jan Valerde | | Department: Billing |
| --- | --- | --- | --- | --- |
| Date | Time In | Time Out | Lunch | Hours Worked |
| Mon. 8/6/12 | 9:00 A.M. | 5:00 P.M. | 0 | 8 |
| Tues. 8/7/12 | 8:30 A.M. | 5:00 P.M. | .50 | 8 |
| Wed. 8/8/12 | 9:30 A.M. | 5:15 P.M. | 1 | 6.75 |
| **Total Hours** | | | | **22.75** |

A. ○ 16
B. ○ 22.75
C. ○ 6.75
D. ○ 8

**4.** After you seal the edges with blue tape, what is the **NEXT** action you should take to prepare a wall for painting?

---

### How to Prepare a Wall for Painting

1. First, remove all pictures, fixtures, and socket and switch covers.

2. Use a lightly dampened rag to remove dust and dirt from walls. Let dry.

3. Next, fill in any holes with sheetrock mud. Let dry.

4. Use large tape to cover edges. Then use blue tape to seal the seam.

5. Finally, place a cloth or plastic tarp on the floor.

---

| A. | ○ | Fill in any holes with sheetrock mud. |
| B. | ○ | Use a lightly dampened rag to clean the wall. |
| C. | ○ | Remove all pictures and fixtures from the wall. |
| D. | ○ | Place a cloth or plastic tarp on the floor. |

**5.** Why should employees of TMO Systems recycle?

---

### TMO Systems Recycling Program

We need your help to meet our goal of reducing trash by 50%. Please place the following items in the blue recycling bins in the cafeteria and break rooms:

| Paper | Plastic | Aluminum | Glass |
|---|---|---|---|
| · Office paper | · Water bottles | · Soda cans | · Glass jars |
| · Newspaper | · Soda bottles | · Soup cans | · Glass bottles |
| · Magazines | · Plastics #1–6 | · Aluminum foil | · (No broken glass) |

Recycling can help TMO Systems meet our goal and help save our planet!

---

| A. | ○ | Because it is mandatory |
| B. | ○ | So the janitors do not have to pick up so much trash |
| C. | ○ | To reduce trash by 50% and help the environment |
| D. | ○ | Because employees will get 50 cents for each item they recycle |

Check your answers on page 167.

 For more Chapter 2 assessment questions, please visit www.mysteckvaughn.com/WORK

# 3 Check and Enhance Comprehension

Monitoring your understanding during and after reading will help you comprehend workplace texts and graphics. In this chapter, you will learn to check your comprehension by identifying the main idea and supporting details of texts and graphics, using context clues, understanding signs and visuals, summarizing, and taking notes.

# Main Idea and Supporting Details

## Build on What You Know

When you tell a friend about an important event in your life, what kinds of details do you include? At the very least, you probably say where you were, who else was there, and what happened. You may also explain when, why, and how the event occurred. These details create a complete picture of the event and help your friend understand the **main idea** of your story.

Details that tell who, what, where, when, why, and how are also important in workplace texts. They tell about the main idea of a document. Whether a document is short and simple or long and complex, locating **supporting details** will help you identify and understand the main idea of what you are reading. Understanding the main idea of workplace documents will help you make good decisions at work and excel at your job. In this lesson, you will practice strategies that will help you locate the main idea and its supporting details in workplace documents.

### In Real Life   Food Safety

Stacey has a job in a restaurant kitchen and just finished preparing some raw seafood for the chef. She has several more dishes to help prepare, including a pasta salad. As she hurries toward the refrigerator to get supplies, she notices the following flyer.

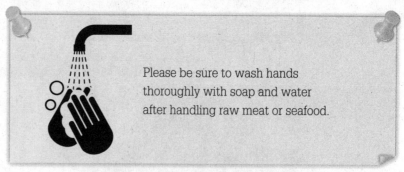

Please be sure to wash hands thoroughly with soap and water after handling raw meat or seafood.

**Discuss the following questions. Share your ideas with the class.**

**1.** What is the main idea of this flyer?

**2.** What should Stacey do before she moves on to her next task?

**3.** What might happen if Stacey does not read or understand this flyer?

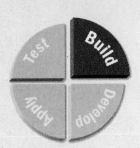

# The 5Ws and H Strategy

You've learned strategies in previous lessons to help you preview and read a document in order to locate its main idea. Sometimes a text's main idea is stated in a heading, in a topic sentence, or in the text's conclusion. Other times, a text's main idea may not be stated. If it's not stated, you can use supporting details from the text to determine the main idea.

Supporting details answer the following questions:

- **Who?** Who is the document about, and who are the intended recipients of the document?

- **What?** What events or actions are described in the document?

- **Where?** What places are mentioned in the document, and why?

- **When?** What dates or times are mentioned in the document, and why?

- **Why?** Why did the author write the document? What is he or she trying to say?

- **How?** If a specific event is described, how did it occur? If a document asks you to do something, how should you proceed?

Keep the 5 Ws and H in mind as you read workplace documents. Doing so will help you quickly locate the most important details and identify the main idea of a document.

 **Take a look at the following meeting invitation. Read each question and discuss your answer with a classmate.**

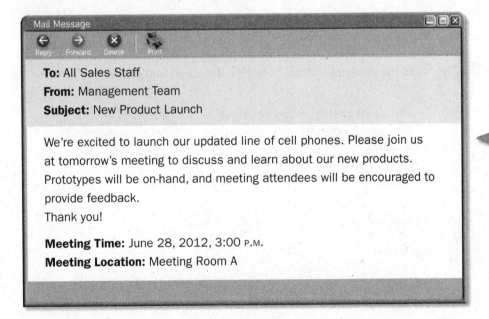

Mail Message

Reply   Forward   Delete   Print

**To:** All Sales Staff
**From:** Management Team
**Subject:** New Product Launch

We're excited to launch our updated line of cell phones. Please join us at tomorrow's meeting to discuss and learn about our new products. Prototypes will be on-hand, and meeting attendees will be encouraged to provide feedback.
Thank you!

**Meeting Time:** June 28, 2012, 3:00 P.M.
**Meeting Location:** Meeting Room A

> **Workplace Tip**
>
> Most workplace documents:
> - Are written for a specific audience
> - Include details that support the main idea

4. What is the main idea of this document?

5. What supporting details can you find using the 5Ws and H strategy?

6. How do the supporting details help you understand the main idea?

# Develop Your Skills

As you complete the activities in this lesson, try to find details in workplace documents that tell who, what, where, when, why, and how.

## Use the 5Ws and H Strategy

Theresa is a veterinary assistant. One of her responsibilities is helping care for the animals. Every day, she receives a new schedule.

 **Look at the schedule and how the 5Ws and H are used.**

| Pet | Feeding Time | Medication |
|-----|--------------|------------|
| Rosie | 9:00/3:00 | 9:00/4:00 |
| Monty | 9:00/3:00 | 12:00 |
| Fox | 9:00/3:00 | 9:00/4:00 |

*Visit animals in their kennels for meals and medication.*

| Who? | Rosie, Monty, and Fox |
|------|------------------------|
| What? | Animals' feeding times and medication |
| Where? | Animal kennels |
| When? | 9:00, 12:00, 3:00, and 4:00 |
| Why? | So animals get their food and medications |
| How? | Theresa should follow the schedule. |

1. What is the main idea of the schedule?

 **Read the following notice. Then fill in the chart and answer the question.**

> **NOTICE:** This building will conduct a fire alarm and emergency exit drill tomorrow at 2:00 P.M. When the alarm sounds, employees should take the stairs to the ground floor and wait in the courtyard until informed that the drill is complete. Thank you.

| 2. Who? | |
|---------|--|
| 3. What? | |
| 4. Where? | |
| 5. When? | |
| 6. Why? | |
| 7. How? | |

8. What is the main idea of the flyer?

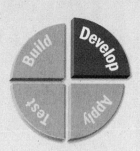

# Locate Main Idea and Supporting Details

You've learned that locating details that tell who, what, where, when, why, and how can be a useful strategy for understanding the main idea. There are also other ways to identify the main idea of a document.

Pay close attention to how a document is organized. As you look for details, make sure to review any headings, topic sentences, graphics, and conclusions. These sections often state or restate the main idea of a workplace document.

 **Read the memo and answer the questions that follow.**

**To:** Company Telemarketers

**From:** Management

**Date:** 7/23/2012

**RE:** Sales Strategies

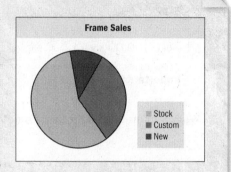

Frame Sales

- Stock
- Custom
- New

This memo is to inform you that the new art and photo frame styles aren't selling as well as anticipated. We believe that outdated catalogues are partly to blame, and we have shipped updated catalogues to our clients. While this will increase visibility, we'd also like our clients to hear more about our new, outstanding products from you.

In the future, when you make sales calls to clients or receive an order by phone, please be sure to mention our new frame styles. If clients place stock or custom frame orders, be sure to recommend comparable items from our new inventory.

Please see your supervisor with questions or concerns. Thank you!

9. Which paragraph tells telemarketers about their new responsibilities?

10. How does the graph help clarify information in the first paragraph?

11. What is the main idea of this memo?

## GOT IT?

**Use strategies to help you locate the main idea and supporting details in a workplace document.**

- Use the 5Ws and H strategy to find details that tell who, what, where, when, why, and how.

- Carefully review headings, topic sentences, graphics, and conclusions to help you identify and understand the main idea.

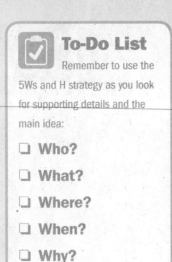

### ✔ To-Do List

Remember to use the
5Ws and H strategy as you look
for supporting details and the
main idea:

❑ **Who?**

❑ **What?**

❑ **Where?**

❑ **When?**

❑ **Why?**

❑ **How?**

# Apply Your Knowledge

Use the strategies you've learned to locate the main idea and supporting details in each workplace document below.

**Read each of the following scenarios and its accompanying document. Select the correct response for each question.**

1. Sara recently started a job as a childcare worker, and she is responsible for helping to look after three toddlers. She received the following schedule.

| Name | Meals | Nap | Medication* |
|------|-------|-----|-------------|
| Mason | 9:00 A.M./12:30 P.M. | 11:00 A.M./2:00 P.M. | None |
| Devon | 9:00 A.M./12:30 P.M. | 11:00 A.M./2:00 P.M. | None |
| Heidi | 9:00 A.M./12:30 P.M. | 11:00 A.M./2:00 P.M. | None |

\* **Important:** Please update if parent provides medication for child.

**What information might Sara sometimes need to update?**

**A.** Meal times

**B.** Nap times

**C.** Medications

**D.** Names of toddlers she looks after

2. What is the main idea of this schedule?

3. Henry works as a library assistant. Part of his job is helping visitors find the books and materials that they need. Construction was recently completed on a new section of the library, and Henry received the following document.

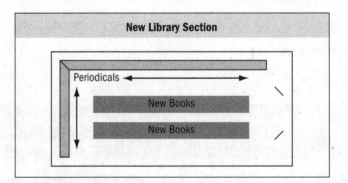

**New Library Section**

Periodicals

New Books

New Books

**Based on the document, Henry should:**

**A.** Send visitors looking for periodicals to the new section of the library.

**B.** Find out what types of books will appear in the new section.

**C.** Send visitors looking for reference materials to the new section.

**D.** Find out if there will be study tables available in the new section.

**4.** You recently got a job helping at an auto mechanic's shop. The shop's owner wants to offer discounts and incentives to help improve business on slow days. He distributed the following document.

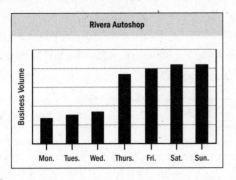

**Rivera Autoshop**

Business Volume

Mon.  Tues.  Wed.  Thurs.  Fri.  Sat.  Sun.

**According to the bar graph, on which day or days should the shop offer incentives?**

**A.** On the weekend

**B.** Monday through Wednesday

**C.** Thursday and Friday

**D.** Sunday

---

**In Real Life** | **Put Your Skills to Work!**

You work for a florist. A movie in which red gerbera daisies are significant is currently very popular in theaters. Your supervisor expects a boost in sales of this type of flower because of the movie. She wants you to create a document that tells customers you have red gerbera daisies in stock and that they are currently marked down.

 **Think about the problem you are facing and put your skills to work! What kind of document would you create and what information would you include? Explain your answers.**

## Think About It!

**Think about the strategies you have practiced in this lesson. How can you use these strategies in your workplace?**

Whether the main idea of a text is stated or unstated, using strategies to find supporting details will help you better understand a workplace document and its main idea. Strategies such as the 5Ws and H will help you locate important details that support the main idea of a document.

**Answer Key**

**1.** C

**2.** The schedule shows what times the children need to be fed, take naps, and take medication.

**3.** A

**4.** B

# Test Your WRC Skills

**Understanding workplace documents requires a variety of reading skills. Read the scenarios and review each document. Select the answer you think best responds to the question.**

1. You work as an aide at a residential care facility. To help you manage your responsibilities, your supervisor has given you the following schedule. According to the schedule, at what time should you update patients' medical records?

| Time | Duty |
|------|------|
| 8:00 A.M.–10:00 A.M. | Update and maintain patient records |
| 10:00 A.M.–12:30 P.M. | Accompany select patients to doctor's appointments and other trips |
| 12:30 P.M.–1:30 P.M. | Lunch break |
| 1:30 P.M.–3:00 P.M. | Replace and launder linens |
| 3:00 P.M.–5:00 P.M. | Visit with, read aloud to, and otherwise entertain patients |

A. ○ 8:00 A.M.–10:00 A.M.

B. ○ 10:00 A.M.–12:30 P.M.

C. ○ 1:30 P.M.–3:00 P.M.

D. ○ 3:00 P.M.–5:00 P.M.

2. According to the flyer, what are all restaurant staff required to wear?

### CAUTION!

All restaurant staff are required to wear slip-resistant footwear. Failure to wear required footwear may lead to accidents and injury.

A. ○ Comfortable footwear

B. ○ Black pants and shirt

C. ○ Slip-resistant footwear

D. ○ Water-resistant uniform

**3.** What is the main idea of this memo?

> **To:** All Employees
> **From:** Management
> **Date:** August 13, 2012
> **Re:** Safety Hazard
>
> This memo is to inform you that employees working in or near Flowers Hall during upcoming renovations must wear respirators and protective clothing until hazardous materials have been cleared from the site. Please see your supervisor with any questions or concerns.

| | | |
|---|---|---|
| **A.** | ○ | Flowers Hall will begin renovation on August 13, 2012. |
| **B.** | ○ | Volunteers are needed to help clear hazardous materials from Flowers Hall. |
| **C.** | ○ | A meeting will take place at Flowers Hall to discuss a new dress code. |
| **D.** | ○ | Employees must wear protective equipment during renovations of Flowers Hall. |

**4.** According to the following policy, what must dry cleaners give a customer when accepting garments?

> 1. Employees **must** provide customer with claim ticket when accepting garments.
> 2. Customers **must** present ticket in order to collect garments.
> 3. If ticket is lost, customer must provide photo ID and sign for garment.

| | | |
|---|---|---|
| **A.** | ○ | Photo ID |
| **B.** | ○ | Claim ticket |
| **C.** | ○ | Signature |
| **D.** | ○ | Garments |

**5.** According to this sign, what should dental assistants do?

> **Remember Your Protective Gloves!**
>
> Dentists and dental assistants are required to wear protective gloves when examining patients or working in exam rooms.

| | | |
|---|---|---|
| **A.** | ○ | Study to become dentists. |
| **B.** | ○ | Wear protective gloves at all times. |
| **C.** | ○ | Ask permission before handling instruments in exam rooms. |
| **D.** | ○ | Wear protective gloves when working in exam rooms. |

Check your
answers on
page 168.

# Use Context Clues

## Build on What You Know

Have you ever come across a word or phrase you didn't know when you
were reading a workplace document? What can you do when this happens?
Often you can use a glossary or dictionary to find a word's meaning,
but what if you don't have a dictionary, or there is no time to look up an
unknown word?

In this lesson, you will learn strategies to help you define unfamiliar words
and phrases you may encounter in workplace documents. You will learn
how to find details that may lead you to the meaning of an unknown word.

**In Real Life** **What's That Word?**

Alex is training for a job as a medical equipment preparer at a
hospital. He will be responsible for sterilizing and maintaining all
machines in his department. The trainer explains that it is important
for Alex to learn how to clean and organize all types of instruments.
Every day he will need to complete the checklist below, but Alex has
never seen the word *autoclave*.

### Daily Tasks

__ Organize surgical equipment trays.

__ Use steam autoclave to sterilize instruments.

__ Update sterilization logs.

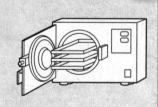

 **Discuss the following questions. Share your ideas with the class.**

**1.** What are some ways that Alex could determine the meaning of the
word *autoclave*?

**2.** Based on Alex's daily tasks, what might *autoclave* mean?

**3.** Is the picture on the checklist important? Why or why not?

**Teacher Reminder**
Review the teacher lesson at
www.mysteckvaughn.com/WORK

**82** Reading

## Why Context Is Important

In Lesson 5, you learned that although you may understand how a document is organized, sometimes you may find difficult or unfamiliar words that you are unsure of in the document. When this happens, you learned that the **context**, or the overall meaning of a document, can help you define the unfamiliar word. You learned to look at the words and phrases surrounding the unfamiliar word to help you define it. You learned to make connections among the graphics, the text, and the overall purpose of a document. When you make these types of connections, you are activating your prior knowledge, building your vocabulary, and improving your comprehension.

## Six Strategies for Finding Meaning

When you need to define an unfamiliar word, you can make connections by searching for valuable context clues. For each type of context clue, you can ask yourself questions as you think about the unfamiliar word:

**Workplace Tip**

You can use context clues to:

• Define unknown words

• Understand a document's purpose

1. **Graphic Aids:** Are there pictures and illustrations near the word?

2. **Definitions:** Is the meaning of the word restated somewhere in the sentence or paragraph?

3. **Synonyms:** Is there a word with a similar meaning that helps explain the unfamiliar word?

4. **Antonyms:** Is there a word with the opposite meaning to compare to the unfamiliar word?

5. **Examples:** Are there words or ideas that give examples of the unknown word?

6. **Word Parts:** Can the word be broken down to determine its meaning?

 **Look at the notice below and discuss the following questions.**

4. Which of the six strategies might you use to figure out the meaning of the word *admittance*?

5. Do you know any additional strategies that may help you find the meaning of a word you do not know?

# Develop Your Skills

Remember, when you encounter an unfamiliar word in a document, the first thing you might do is scan the document for helpful graphics. When there are no graphic aids, your next step should be to look for other clues.

## Definitions and Examples

Sometimes a definition or restatement of an unfamiliar word will be in the same sentence or paragraph. Similarly, workplace texts often include examples that can help you figure out what a word means. To locate a definition or example, you can look for these clue words and phrases:

| Definition Clues: | or | which is | refers to | means |
|---|---|---|---|---|
| Example Clues: | for example | like | such as | for instance |

 **Read the document below. Then answer the questions that follow.**

> **To: Produce Clerks**
> **Please check sell-by dates on a daily basis. All *outdated* produce, such as expired salad greens, must be removed from the shelves. These items must be placed in the compost *receptacle*, which is the green container near the back door.**

1. What is the example for the word *outdated*?

2. Is there a definition clue for the word *receptacle*?

3. How do these clues help you understand the meaning of the document?

## Synonym and Antonym Clues

In addition to definitions and examples, you can often find a word near the unfamiliar word that has the same or the opposite meaning. A nearby **synonym**, a word with a similar meaning, or an **antonym**, a word with the opposite meaning, may provide a hint about the unfamiliar word.

 **With a classmate, work together to decide whether each italicized word has an antonym or synonym clue. Then list the word or phrase that is the antonym or synonym.**

4. Although Raul thought the test would be *arduous,* it was quite easy.

5. Marco gave *explicit*, clear directions so Jim could follow them easily.

6. You need to clean up the *debris*, including the garbage near the front.

7. The diagrams in the manual were *vague*, but Keesha was able to clarify which tools she needed to fix the machine.

# Using Word Parts as Clues

Sometimes identifying the parts of an unfamiliar word can give you ideas about its meaning. You can separate some words into parts. A **prefix** may be added to the beginning of a word, or a **suffix** may be added to the end of a word. Then you can identify the **root**, which is the base word that remains after you remove any prefixes and suffixes.

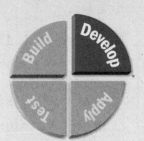

| Common Prefixes | Common Suffixes |
| --- | --- |
| un-, in-, dis-, mis- | -ful, -ly, -able, -ous |

 **Break the following words into their word parts. Write the root word and the prefix or suffix.**

| | PREFIX | ROOT | SUFFIX |
| --- | --- | --- | --- |
| **8.** Disagree | | | |
| **9.** Harmful | | | |
| **10.** Unstoppable | | | |

 **Read the following note and answer the question that follows.**

> Irma,
>
> I think it is *hazardous* to store the copy paper near the fire exits. Please move all paper to the shelves in Storage Room A.
>
> -Thanks, Kevin

**11.** How can breaking down *hazardous* help you understand its meaning?

## Substitution Strategy

When you have an idea of what an unfamiliar word might mean, try substituting your idea for the unfamiliar word. Reread the sentence with the word, and see if it makes sense. You may need to try more than one strategy before you find a word or phrase that makes sense.

| GOT IT? | When you encounter a word you don't know, remember to: |
| --- | --- |

- Search the text around the word for clues about what it means.
- When possible, break a word down and identify its smaller parts.
- Check your idea for the unknown word to see if it makes sense.

# Apply Your Knowledge

Defining unfamiliar words requires that you search for clues in the words and sentences that surround them.

**Read each scenario. Then select the correct response for each question.**

1. Yesterday you submitted your first time sheet at your new job. When you arrived at work this morning, you found this note from the payroll clerk.

> There is a discrepancy on your time sheet. The number of hours you listed does not match the schedule submitted by your supervisor. Please come to my office so we can correct this error.

**Based on the information in this note, a *discrepancy* is:**

A. A delay

B. An inconsistency

C. A warning

D. An interruption

2. Which words help you understand the meaning of the word *discrepancy*?

A. Does not match

B. Come to my office

C. Submitted by your supervisor

D. On your time sheet

3. It is Steve's first day of training at a restaurant. When he arrives at work, his co-worker asks for help with this task list before lunch.

> 1. **Wipe all countertops.**
>
> 2. **Sweep under chairs and tables.**
>
> 3. **Clean all condiment trays.**
>
> 4. **Fill condiment trays with ketchup and mustard packets.**
>
> 5. **Empty trash cans into the dumpster.**

**Based on the information in this task list, the word *condiment* refers to:**

A. Chairs and tables

B. Ketchup and mustard packets

C. Countertops

D. Trash cans

4. Your boss asks you to mail an important package to a client in London. You go to the mailroom, but it is closed. You call your boss and leave a voicemail about the problem. At work the next day, you see this e-mail from your boss.

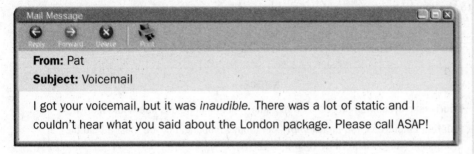

| Mail Message |
| --- |

**From:** Pat

**Subject:** Voicemail

I got your voicemail, but it was *inaudible*. There was a lot of static and I couldn't hear what you said about the London package. Please call ASAP!

**Based on the information in this e-mail, the word *inaudible* means:**

**A.** Impossible to see

**B.** Easy to see

**C.** Impossible to hear

**D.** Easy to hear

## In Real Life    Put Your Skills to Work!

You just start working in the warehouse of a paper company. Your supervisor tells you the importance of using heavy machinery safely and not misusing the trash baler. You are unsure of what the word *misusing* means, and you see this sign on the trash baler.

> **CAUTION!**
>
> *Misuse* of this machine can result in bodily harm or death.

 **Think about the problem you are facing and put your skills to work! Explain how you might figure out the meaning of the unknown word.**

**Workplace Tip**

Which types of clues can help you understand the sign?

## Think About It!

How might using context clues help you understand workplace texts?

Using strategies to define unfamiliar words can help you read faster and build your vocabulary. Finding context clues can help you make connections between the ideas in a document, which will also help you understand the overall meaning.

**Answer Key**

**1.** B

**2.** A

**3.** B

**4.** C

# Test Your WRC Skills

**Defining an unfamiliar word in a text requires that you look for clues about the word's meaning. Read the following scenarios and review each document. Select the answer you think best responds to the question.**

**1.** In the context of this notice, what is the meaning of the word *exempt*?

---

**NOTICE**

**Hourly Employees:** You must attend the time sheet meeting this afternoon at 2 P.M.

**Salaried Employees:** You are *exempt* from today's meeting, but you must attend the overtime meeting tomorrow at 10 A.M.

---

| | | |
|---|---|---|
| **A.** | ○ | To earn a salary |
| **B.** | ○ | To attend a meeting |
| **C.** | ○ | To sign a time sheet |
| **D.** | ○ | To be excused |

**2.** What are *modifications*?

| **Regular Hours** | | **Holiday Hours** | |
|---|---|---|---|
| Monday | 9 A.M.–7 P.M. | Monday | 9 A.M.–9 P.M. |
| Tuesday | 9 A.M.–7 P.M. | Tuesday | 9 A.M.–9 P.M. |
| Wednesday | 9 A.M.–7 P.M. | Wednesday | 8 A.M.–10 P.M. |
| Thursday | 9 A.M.–7 P.M. | Thursday | 8 A.M.–10 P.M. |
| Friday | 9 A.M.–7 P.M. | Friday | 8 A.M.–11 P.M. |
| Saturday | 9 A.M.–8 P.M. | Saturday | 8 A.M.–11 P.M. |
| Sunday | 9 A.M.–5 P.M. | Sunday | 8 A.M.–6 P.M. |

All employees must take note of the *modifications* to store hours during the upcoming holidays. These changes will allow each employee to work up to ten hours of overtime per week.

| | | |
|---|---|---|
| **A.** | ○ | Holidays |
| **B.** | ○ | Changes |
| **C.** | ○ | Questions |
| **D.** | ○ | Store hours |

**3.** What is the meaning of the word *confidential*?

> **From:** l.chung@xyz.com
>
> **Subject:** Classified Information
>
> It has come to my attention that some employees have been sharing information about their sales with some of our customers. This information is strictly *confidential* and should not be shared with anyone outside of our company. Sharing information about your sales is a serious offense!

| | | |
|---|---|---|
| **A.** | ◯ | Private |
| **B.** | ◯ | Illegal |
| **C.** | ◯ | Angry |
| **D.** | ◯ | Offensive |

**4.** In the context of this welcome letter, what is the meaning of the word *acquaint*?

> **WELCOME ALL NEW EMPLOYEES!**
>
> I want to welcome each of you to our company. I am excited that you are part of our team! Please *acquaint* yourself with the Safety in the Workplace chapter of your employee handbook before tomorrow's meeting. It is very important that you get to know all of our safety policies and procedures. If you are not familiar with these policies, you will not be prepared for the meeting.

| | | |
|---|---|---|
| **A.** | ◯ | To be welcomed |
| **B.** | ◯ | To be safe |
| **C.** | ◯ | To get to know |
| **D.** | ◯ | To be part of a team |

**5.** What is the meaning of *unlawful*?

> **WARNING:**
>
> *Unlawful* use of machines in Section A is prohibited!
> You must have a permit to use all machines in this area.

| | | |
|---|---|---|
| **A.** | ◯ | Not safe |
| **B.** | ◯ | Not legal |
| **C.** | ◯ | Not finished |
| **D.** | ◯ | Not working |

Check your answers on page 168.

# Understand Signs and Visuals

## Build on What You Know

As you traveled to work or class today, how many signs did you see along the road? Did you see any of the following?

Signs are everywhere: on the roadside, in stores, at work, and even in your own home. Signs can guide you to the correct location, warn you about problems you may encounter, give you directions, or even explain how to complete a specific project or activity. Signs are like text messages: short, to the point, and targeted to specific audiences. Being able to interpret signs is an important life skill and may, in some cases, protect you from injury or even save your life.

In this lesson, you will learn strategies that will help you interpret the signs that you encounter at home, in your community, and in the workplace.

### In Real Life    What Sign?

Returning late from lunch and worrying that she would miss the weekly conference call with her supervisor, Janice walked quickly down the hallway to her cubicle. Thinking ahead about the conference call, Janice missed a new sign that had been posted in the hallway while she was at lunch. As she rounded the corner, her cell phone rang, and she leaned against the wall to answer it.

 **With a classmate, discuss the following questions. Share your ideas with the class.**

1. Why was the sign posted?

2. What happened to Janice when she leaned against the wall?

3. How could Janice avoid this problem in the future?

## Interpreting Texts

In Lessons 1 and 2, you learned about different types of texts and some basic strategies to use whenever you read. You learned to:

- **Preview** the text to see what it is about.

- **Identify** what you want to know or learn.

- **Read** through the introduction to predict the main idea.

- **Look** for details that support the main idea.

- **Summarize** what you have read.

## Interpreting Signs and Visuals

The steps you take to interpret signs or other **visuals** are very similar to those you learned for interpreting text. You need to:

1. **Skim** to get the "big picture."

2. **Ask** what you need to know or learn from the sign.

3. **Identify** any symbol or object that you already know.

4. **Scan** and locate any key words or specific colors that are used.

5. **Confirm** that you have all the information you need to understand the sign or visual.

**Take a look at the sign below. Then read each question and see if you have a similar response to the one provided.**

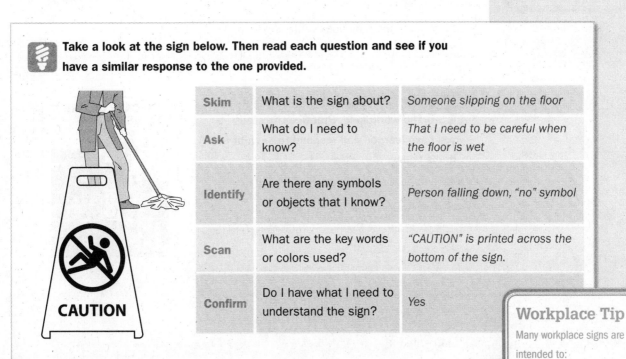

| | | |
|---|---|---|
| Skim | What is the sign about? | *Someone slipping on the floor* |
| Ask | What do I need to know? | *That I need to be careful when the floor is wet* |
| Identify | Are there any symbols or objects that I know? | *Person falling down, "no" symbol* |
| Scan | What are the key words or colors used? | *"CAUTION" is printed across the bottom of the sign.* |
| Confirm | Do I have what I need to understand the sign? | *Yes* |

4. Why might your employer post this sign? Share your ideas with the class.

**Workplace Tip**

Many workplace signs are intended to:

- Prevent injuries

- Make the work environment as safe as possible

# Develop Your Skills

Remember, to understand a sign or visual, you need to complete the five-step process: skim, ask, identify, scan, and confirm.

## Steps to Interpreting Signs

Look at the sign and how each of the five steps is completed.

> ### Authorized Personnel Only
>
> Badge Required for Entry!

| Skim | What is the sign about? | Who can enter an area |
| --- | --- | --- |
| Ask | What do I need to know? | If I can enter the area |
| Identify | Are there any symbols or objects that I know? | An exclamation point |
| Scan | What are the key words or colors used? | Authorized personnel, badge required |
| Confirm | Do I have what I need to understand the sign? | Yes |

**1.** What is the main idea of the sign?

> ### Workplace Tip
>
> Being aware of the colors in a sign is an important part of interpreting its correct meaning. Remember that red means stop, and yellow means caution.

The following sign is often found in the workplace. Practice the steps you have learned and respond to each of the items below.

IN CASE OF FIRE
USE STAIRS

| 2. | Skim | |
| --- | --- | --- |
| 3. | Ask | |
| 4. | Identify | |
| 5. | Scan | |
| 6. | Confirm | |

**7.** What is the main idea of the sign?

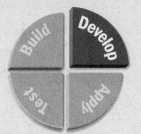

# Different Types of Signs in the Workplace

Understanding the different types of signs and why they are posted can help you interpret them correctly and determine what they are telling you to do. In the workplace, you may encounter the following types of signs:

- **Directional signs** show you where something is located or how to get to a specific place.

- **Health and safety signs** warn you about hazards, tell you what to do in an emergency, or explain how to protect yourself from injury.

- **Informational signs** tell you about a meeting or provide an update on something that you already know.

- **Instructional signs** tell you how to perform a specific task.

 **Look at the following signs and check the appropriate category for each.**

**8.**
> Employees must wash hands for at least 20 seconds before returning to work.

- ❏ Directional
- ❏ Health and Safety
- ❏ Informational
- ❏ Instructional

**9.**
> # EMERGENCY EXIT

- ❏ Directional
- ❏ Health and Safety
- ❏ Informational
- ❏ Instructional

**10.**
> **NOTICE!**
> All Employees:
> Meeting at 3:00 P.M. on Thursday

- ❏ Directional
- ❏ Health and Safety
- ❏ Informational
- ❏ Instructional

**GOT IT?** | **Understanding signs and visuals is important. When you see a sign:**

- Think about what you need to know.
- Check out the features of the sign.
- Make sure you have all the information you need.
- Use the information to determine what to do.

**Answer Key**

1. Authorized personnel must show their badges to enter the area.
2. What to do in case of a fire
3. That I need to use stairs if there is a fire
4. "No" symbol, picture of fire, stairs
5. Fire, use stairs
6. Yes, I have what I need to understand the sign.
7. Use the stairs instead of the elevator if there is a fire.
8. Instructional or Health and Safety
9. Directional or Health and Safety
10. Informational

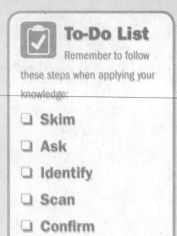

**To-Do List**

Remember to follow these steps when applying your knowledge:

❑ **Skim**

❑ **Ask**

❑ **Identify**

❑ **Scan**

❑ **Confirm**

# Apply Your Knowledge

Interpreting signs requires that you complete a five-step process.

**Read each of the following scenarios and interpret its accompanying sign. Select the correct response for each question.**

1.  Maxie just started working at a construction firm. Most of the time she manages files, answers phones, and maintains schedules. She may have to visit a job site, but she hasn't done so yet. Yesterday, she noticed her boss take the following sign out to a job site.

    > NO ENTRY TO JOB SITE WITHOUT
    > PROPER SAFETY GEAR.
    > NO EXCEPTIONS!

    **Based on the information in the sign, Maxie will:**

    **A.** Need to wear a hard hat, boots, and gloves any time she visits a job site.

    **B.** Need to start wearing a hard hat to work every day.

    **C.** Need to ask her supervisor what she should do.

    **D.** Not worry about the sign since she always works in the office.

2.  What type of sign did Maxie's boss take to the job site?

3.  Wayne is looking for a job at the new shipping warehouse. He has always worked hard, shown up on time, and worked extra shifts when needed. Wayne can drive a forklift, operate heavy equipment, and has good computer skills. However, he doesn't have a college degree and is worried that he might not qualify for certain jobs. Wayne sees the following sign:

    > **ABC Express Shipping & Warehouse**
    > **Now Hiring**
    >
    > · High school diploma or equivalent required
    > · Must be able to operate forklift
    > · Must have basic computer skills
    > · Must be willing to work midnight to 8 A.M.
    > Applications due on 7/15

    **Based on the information included in the sign, Wayne:**

    **A.** Will not be able to apply for the job because of the schedule.

    **B.** Does not meet the computer skills requirement.

    **C.** Has all the necessary qualifications for the job.

    **D.** Should call and ask if he is qualified to apply for the job.

**4.** You have to deliver boxes of food to a restaurant. When you arrive at the restaurant, there is only one employee available. He tells you to leave the boxes near the back door. When you look above the back door, you notice the following sign.

---

**EMERGENCY EXIT**
**Do Not Block**

---

**Based on the information in the sign, you should:**

**A.** Leave the boxes by the door as suggested.

**B.** Take the boxes back to the delivery center.

**C.** Tell the employee to move the boxes later.

**D.** Help the employee locate a better location for the boxes.

---

**In Real Life** **Put Your Skills to Work!**

Your boss has serious concerns about copier costs. Recently, the monthly maintenance fee for copiers has jumped more than 25 percent, yet he knows that there have been no big copy jobs for the company. He wants you to create a sign that can be posted over the copier to inform people that they cannot use work copiers for personal use. Develop a sign as your boss requested.

 **Think about the problem you are facing and put your skills to work! What kind of sign would you create? Explain your reasons.**

**Workplace Tip**

When creating your sign, think about:

• The purpose of the sign

• Using key words or colors

• Using symbols or images

---

**Think About It!**

**What information could you get from the signs posted at your workplace?**

Signs are important in workplace settings. Important information, such as fire exits, washing your hands before returning to work, and even how to clock in to work, is often provided through signs and visuals.

**Answer Key**

**1.** A

**2.** Health and Safety

**3.** C

**4.** D

# Test Your WRC Skills

**Interpreting signs and visuals requires a variety of reading skills. Read the following scenarios and review each sign and visual. Select the answer you think best responds to the question.**

1. Your company has recently launched an employee health campaign to help reduce insurance costs. This sign is now seen throughout company headquarters and will soon be distributed to all branch locations. What is the main idea of the sign?

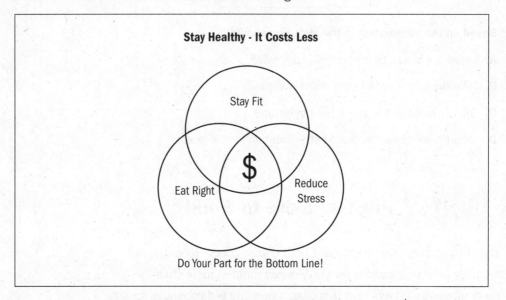

| | | |
|---|---|---|
| **A.** | ○ | Start dieting and exercising today or your pay will be decreased. |
| **B.** | ○ | Healthy employees help the company reduce costs. |
| **C.** | ○ | Employees who have poor eating habits will be fired. |
| **D.** | ○ | All employees should watch what they eat and exercise to reduce stress. |

2. Why would a company most likely post a sign such as the following?

| | | |
|---|---|---|
| **A.** | ○ | To reduce costs for supplies |
| **B.** | ○ | To prevent spills |
| **C.** | ○ | To prevent employee injuries |
| **D.** | ○ | To make sure the right supplies are used for certain jobs |

3. According to this sign, what should employees do when the office machines don't work properly?

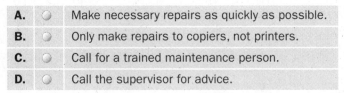

**For copier repairs, call: 555-555-1000.**

| A. | ○ | Make necessary repairs as quickly as possible. |
| B. | ○ | Only make repairs to copiers, not printers. |
| C. | ○ | Call for a trained maintenance person. |
| D. | ○ | Call the supervisor for advice. |

4. What is the main purpose of this sign?

> Mandatory Meeting – Health Insurance Update
> Tuesday, October 12
>
> 9:00–10:00
>
> Meeting Rooms B and C

| A. | ○ | To encourage employees to buy health insurance |
| B. | ○ | To announce a required meeting for all employees |
| C. | ○ | To discuss mandatory health insurance coverage for all employees |
| D. | ○ | To let employees know that Meeting Rooms B and C will be in use |

**Check your answers on page 169.**

# Summarize

## Build on What You Know

When your friend asks "What did you do this weekend?" you probably don't answer by giving an hour-by-hour account. Your friend doesn't want to know every detail—what time you woke up, how long you watched TV, when you brushed your teeth, and so on. Instead, you give a **summary**, or a brief account of the main ideas and important details.

You will likely do a lot of summarizing in the workplace. For example, a co-worker might ask you to give a quick **synopsis** of what she missed in the training session last week, or you might be required to give a client a summary of your company's services. This lesson will show you why summarizing is useful and teach you effective ways to do it.

### In Real Life     Wait a Minute!

Chloe works as an administrative assistant at a small law firm. She has just received a copy of the agenda for today's committee meeting. Chloe sees that she is responsible for summarizing the last meeting's **minutes**, so she reviews the following document before the meeting.

> **Committee Meeting Minutes**
>
> **Meeting Date:** January 24, 2012
> · The meeting was called to order at 3:00 in the main boardroom.
> **Attendees:** Chloe Morgan, Dorothy Ramirez, Mark O'Neil, Emily Tau
> **Approval of Previous Minutes**
> · All minutes from the January 20 meeting were approved by vote.
> **Business Arising from the Minutes**
> · Topic: Automatic soap dispensers in the bathrooms
> · Dorothy proposed that automatic soap dispensers would save money. Mark believed the installation would be too costly.
> **Motion:** The committee has agreed to do a cost-analysis for the installation of automatic soap dispensers.

**Discuss the following questions. Share your ideas with the class.**

1. How can Chloe use the above document to help her summarize?

2. What kinds of information should Chloe include in her summary?

3. Why is summarizing the last meeting's minutes important?

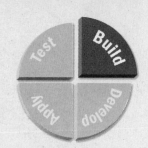

## What Is Summarizing?

In Lesson 7 you learned that identifying the main idea and supporting details in workplace documents can help you understand what you read. Summarizing is another strategy you can use to better comprehend workplace documents.

A summary is just a brief review of the main ideas and important details told in your own words. It's the basic gist of a document.

## Reasons to Summarize

Summarizing is a very useful strategy in the workplace. It can help you:

1. **Improve your understanding.**

   You will know that you understood what you read if you are able to identify the main idea and key details to create a summary. You should be able to answer questions like "What was this procedure document about?" or "Did I understand the main ideas in this memo?" Summarizing is an excellent way to confirm your comprehension of any workplace document.

2. **Recall what you read.**

   Remembering what you read at work is important. For example, you may be required to recall information from an e-mail, a policy, or a manual. If you take time to summarize what you read, you will have a much easier time remembering it later.

3. **Inform others.**

   In your job, you may be asked to provide a summary so that others can understand basic information. Whether this information is for a co-worker, a client, or a supervisor, the ability to summarize shows that you can determine what is important to share with others and that you can present it in a way that is brief and to the point.

 **Read the following scenarios and determine the reason for summarizing.**

4. Nao has just begun working as a plumber's assistant. He is reading a chapter in a manual about safety regulations. He is confused by all the information, so he decides to summarize each section.

5. You work as a home health aide for the elderly and must keep a log of what you do each day with your clients. At the end of the week, you submit a summary of your log entries to your supervisor.

6. You have just finished reading a lengthy explanation of your health benefits. You write a summary on a sticky note so that you won't forget the important points.

# Develop Your Skills

Now that you know what summarizing is and some reasons to summarize in the workplace, you can explore useful tips and techniques to help you summarize effectively.

## Summarizing Basics

People use different techniques to summarize, but all summaries follow a few simple rules. Here are some basic tips to remember when you summarize workplace documents.

- **Make it short:** A summary is always shorter than the original document.

- **Focus only on the main ideas and key details:** Leave out anything that does not directly relate to the main ideas or key details, such as long descriptions or repeated information.

- **Use your own words:** When you restate something in your own words, it helps you understand it better. It can also help you remember the information and communicate it to others.

- **Don't add new ideas:** A summary only contains information from the original document. When you add information or personal opinions, you are no longer summarizing.

**Read the following scenario and discuss the question with a classmate.**

A customer at an electronics store is looking through a product catalog. He is confused by the information provided about big screen TVs. He asks Natasha, a store employee, to summarize the information. Natasha uses the catalog to read almost all of the information back to the customer, and she gives a long explanation that includes her own opinions about the product.

1. Determine whether Natasha's summary was successful in meeting its purpose, and why.

> **Workplace Tip**
> A summary can give customers the basic information they need to make an informed decision.

## That's Out of Sight!

One technique to help you summarize involves reading a document or section of a document, placing it out of sight, and then creating a summary based only on what you can remember. Usually the most important main ideas and key details will remain in your mind, while everything else will fade. When you finish summarizing, check the document again to make sure that nothing important was forgotten.

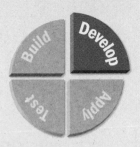

 **Read the following document, and then cover it with a piece of paper. Answer the questions below.**

### Notice to Employees

Please do not leave food in the refrigerator overnight. There have been several complaints of rotten items on the shelves. Not only is this inconsiderate, it is unsanitary. All unclaimed food will now be thrown away every Friday at 5:00.

**2.** What are the main idea and key details from the notice?

**3.** Create a summary from memory.

## The Shrinking Summary

A summary might be one sentence or an entire paragraph. It depends on the size of the document and the purpose of the summary. If you have a lengthy document, summarize each paragraph separately. Then combine the mini-summaries to make an even smaller, more concise summary.

 **Read the following document and answer the questions.**

---

#### Company Vehicle Policy

**Driver Responsibilities:** Company drivers must complete a defensive driving course, submit a clean driving record, and hold a valid driver's license. Drivers must follow all state and local traffic laws, as well as the company rules set forth in this policy.

**Vehicle Inspection and Maintenance:** Drivers are responsible for regularly inspecting the cleanliness and overall condition of company vehicles. Transportation managers are required to arrange all preventive and repair maintenance.

**Accident Report Procedure:** Use the following procedure in the event of an accident:

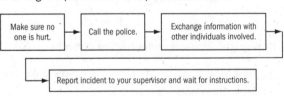

---

**4.** How would you summarize each section of this policy?

**5.** How would you summarize the policy as a whole?

---

**GOT IT?** **Summarize to better understand, remember, and communicate what you read. When summarizing:**

- Make it short.
- Use your own words.
- Focus on the main ideas and key details.
- Don't add new ideas.

# Apply Your Knowledge

Summarizing can help you understand, remember, and share what you read. Use the tips and techniques you learned to summarize successfully.

**Read each of the following scenarios and preview the documents. Select the correct response for each question.**

1. Before beginning work as a salesperson at a department store, Taylor is given some informational materials to review. She finds and reads the following letter.

> Dear New Employee:
>
> Welcome to the Morgan team! As you know, Morgan offers an enormous product selection. Our clothing department makes up the biggest percentage of our inventory and provides the largest income. We encourage all employees to familiarize themselves with the brands and locations of items in this department. Our shoe department is our second largest inventory, followed by our kitchen, bathroom, and beauty departments. Employees should know the locations of these departments and what kinds of products are offered there.
>
> **Flooor Plan**
>
> Kitchen
> Clothing
> Bath
> Restroom
> Shoes
> Beauty
>
> It is essential that our employees know what kinds of products our store carries so that we can assist customers and promote sales. Contact your manager with any questions regarding store inventory.
>
> Thank you,
>
> The Morgan Management Team

**How might Taylor summarize the letter?**

**A.** New Morgan employees need to know the brand and exact location of every item in the store.

**B.** New Morgan employees must only become familiar with inventory in the department where they will work.

**C.** New Morgan employees should memorize the clothing department inventory because it is the store's biggest money-maker.

**D.** New Morgan employees should become familiar with the store's inventory and layout so they can help customers and make sales.

2. Why would Taylor summarize the letter?

3. It is a slow day at the bookstore. You are a sales floor assistant and know that if you are not helping people locate the books they need, you should help put books away. When you go to get the book cart, you notice the following document taped to the side.

---

**Shelving Reminder**

In addition to shelving the books on the cart, please make sure that the books on the bookshelves are correctly ordered and neatly arranged. It is common for bookstore patrons to reshelve books in the wrong places.

---

**Based on the document, what should you remember to do?**

**A.** Remind the bookstore patrons to shelve books correctly and neatly.

**B.** Make sure books on the shelf are in the right order and neatly arranged.

**C.** Shelve books on the cart and don't worry about the books on the shelf.

**D.** Tidy up the books on the shelf instead of shelving the books on the cart.

4. Which information in the reminder would not be included in a summary?

## In Real Life | Put Your Skills to Work!

Your manager at the restaurant where you work doesn't understand why the night staff is not following the closing procedure. You feel that the procedure document is too long and difficult to follow. Each step has a lot of extra details and repetitive language. You volunteer to make a poster that summarizes the important points.

 **Think about the problem you are facing and put your skills to work! What techniques will you use to summarize the closing procedure? What kinds of information will you include in your summary?**

**Workplace Tip**

When creating your poster, think about:

- The reason why you are writing the summary
- Summarizing each step in the procedure separately
- Including only the most important information

## Think About It!

**In what ways might summarizing be useful to you in the workplace?**

Summarizing is an effective strategy to help you understand and remember what you read. It can also be a useful way to briefly communicate a lot of information. Summarizing techniques, such as recalling information from memory or summarizing a large document section by section, can improve your ability to summarize well.

**Answer Key**

**1.** D

**2.** To make sure she understands the letter and to remember what it says

**3.** B

**4.** It is common for bookstore patrons to reshelve books in the wrong places.

# Test Your WRC Skills

**Summarizing can help you better comprehend what you read. Read the following scenarios and review each document. Select the answer you think best responds to the question.**

**1.** According to this sign, what might happen if you climb a ladder carrying tools in your hand?

# DON'T FALL!

**Carry all tools in your tool belt.**

| | | |
|---|---|---|
| **A.** | ○ | You might need a new ladder. |
| **B.** | ○ | You might wear a tool belt. |
| **C.** | ○ | You might fall off the ladder. |
| **D.** | ○ | You might forget your tools. |

**2.** Based on this e-mail, what is being requested?

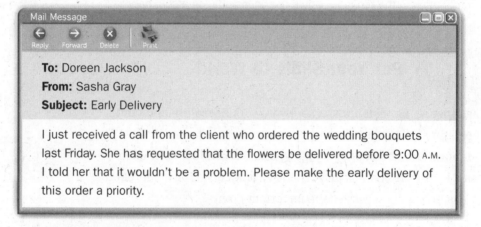

Mail Message

Reply    Forward    Delete    Print

**To:** Doreen Jackson
**From:** Sasha Gray
**Subject:** Early Delivery

I just received a call from the client who ordered the wedding bouquets last Friday. She has requested that the flowers be delivered before 9:00 A.M. I told her that it wouldn't be a problem. Please make the early delivery of this order a priority.

| | | |
|---|---|---|
| **A.** | ○ | An early flower delivery |
| **B.** | ○ | An order of wedding bouquets |
| **C.** | ○ | A call to the client |
| **D.** | ○ | An early wedding |

**3.** According to this sign, who is allowed to use the freight elevator?

**Authorized Personnel Only**

No tenants or guests are allowed on the freight elevator at any time. Only authorized personnel are allowed on the freight elevator. Please contact building management to arrange for large deliveries.

| | | |
|---|---|---|
| **A.** | ○ | Guests |
| **B.** | ○ | Tenants |
| **C.** | ○ | Authorized personnel |
| **D.** | ○ | Building management |

**4.** According to this survey, what is the overall satisfaction of this customer?

### Customer Satisfaction Survey
Thank you for choosing the Lion's Den Lodge.
Please take a moment to let us know how you enjoyed your stay.

| | Very Satisfied | Satisfied | Somewhat Satisfied | Not Satisfied |
|---|---|---|---|---|
| **Comfort** | X | | | |
| **Cleanliness** | X | | | |
| **Staff** | X | | | |
| **Food** | | X | | |
| **Price** | X | | | |

**Comments:** <u>We loved our stay! The view from our window was breathtaking.</u>
<u>Roberto at the front desk gave us wonderful sightseeing recommendations.</u>
<u>We plan to come back soon!</u>

**A.** ○ Not satisfied
**B.** ○ Somewhat satisfied
**C.** ○ Satisfied
**D.** ○ Very satisfied

**5.** Based on this document, what holidays will all employees have off?

### Bank Holidays

Full-time employees will receive paid time off on bank holidays. Part-time and temporary employees will not receive pay but are not expected to work. Our bank observes the following holidays. Additional days off must be requested in advance and approved by your supervisor.

· New Year's Day
· Martin Luther King, Jr. Day
· Memorial Day
· Independence Day
· Labor Day
· Thanksgiving Day
· Christmas Day

**A.** ○ No holidays
**B.** ○ Bank holidays
**C.** ○ Religious holidays
**D.** ○ All holidays

**Check your answers on page 169.**

# Skills for the Workplace

## Note Taking

When you were in school, you probably took notes from a textbook and then used those notes to study for a test. In the workplace, people take notes to help them understand what they are reading. Taking notes helps you focus on the information at hand, as well as identify the main ideas or most important points. Ask yourself, *Is this important enough to write in my notes?* Notes also help you remember the most important information. You are more likely to remember the things you write down, and your notes can provide a useful reference when you are trying to remember the information later.

Even if you never took notes in school, you can learn to take **effective** notes in the workplace. Use these tips to help you:

- Write down only the most important ideas. These are the things you need to *know* and the things you need to *do*. Using the 5Ws and H questions can help you identify the most important information.

- Organize your notes in a way that works for you. Some people divide a piece of paper into three parts: things to know, things to do, and questions. Another way is to draw a small box next to each item you need to do later. Then check off each box as you complete the item.

- If the document belongs to you, write on it! Use a highlighter or underline the most important points. Write down your questions right away so you don't forget to ask them later.

- Use a calendar. When you read about a meeting, training session, or due date, write it down immediately in your calendar. Check your calendar frequently so you do not miss any important dates.

## Workplace Scenario

> **MEMO**
>
> **To:** All hotel clerks
> **From:** Management
> **RE:** Mandatory training session
>
> As a condition of our insurance policy, all hotel clerks are required to attend a training session on handling emergency situations. The training session will take place next Monday at 1:00 in Meeting Room C. Bring writing materials and your photo ID.

- What important information would you highlight or write down? *The subject of the training; the date, time, location, and what to bring*

# Workplace Practice

**Mail Message**

**To:** All employees
**From:** Human Resources
**Subject:** Badge-in, badge-out system

You may have noticed the new badge readers at all entrances and exits. Starting next Monday, you must use your identification badge every time you enter and exit the facility. This badge-in, badge-out system will provide better security for our work areas. For your safety, it will be disabled in the case of a fire alarm or other emergency.

Additionally, employees will no longer need to complete a weekly time sheet. Instead, your hours will be calculated automatically. If you misplace your badge or forget to badge in or out, please contact Human Resources as soon as possible.

**Workplace Tip**

It is a good practice to take notes on any changes to your work tasks or procedures. Which employee would you promote: one who understands and follows directions the first time or one who always needs to be reminded?

- What is the most important information you need to know?
  *Starting on Monday, you will need to use your identification badge to enter and exit the building.*

- What will you need to do differently? *You will need to use a badge to enter and exit. You will not need to fill out a time sheet. You will need to contact Human Resources if you misplace your badge or forget to use it.*

- What would happen if you did not read, understand, or remember the information in this e-mail? *You might not be paid for all your hours.*

## It's Your Turn!

1. Your boss asks you to work an extra shift next Tuesday. What should you do to make sure you remember?

2. You receive a description of three health insurance plans. You don't understand how they are alike and how they are different. What could you do to help you understand?

3. You are a new employee at a hospital switchboard. Your supervisor gives you a booklet about patient confidentiality and tells you it is important to understand what you can and cannot reveal about patients. How might taking notes help you in this situation?

4. A new employee will join your department next week. Your boss gives you a safety manual and asks you to fill in the new employee on the most important safety information. How might taking notes help you in this situation?

*It's Your Turn!* **Answer Key**
**1.** Write it on your calendar.
**2.** Write down the most important information about each one and compare them to each other.
**3.** Taking notes can help you identify the most important information. It might also help you come up with questions for your supervisor.
**4.** Taking notes can help you identify the most important information and share it with the new employee.

# Chapter 3 Assessment

**Select the answer you think best responds to the question.**

**1.** What does the word *minimum* mean?

### Required Cooking Temperatures for Serving

| Type of Food | Minimum Internal Temperature (°F) |
|---|---|
| Poultry, stuffed meats | 165° for 15 seconds |
| Ground beef, pork | 160° for 15 seconds |
| Seafood, steaks, and eggs | 145° for 15 seconds |

A. ○ Raw
B. ○ Lowest
C. ○ Starting
D. ○ Highest

**2.** You are looking for a place to store your lunch and find a refrigerator with this sign. What should you do?

**⚠ WARNING**
**Biohazard**
No food or drink
to be stored in
this refrigerator

A. ○ You should put your lunch in this refrigerator.
B. ○ You should throw away your lunch because it could be contaminated.
C. ○ You should look for another place to store your lunch.
D. ○ You should not bring your lunch to this job site.

**3.** According to the policy, can you shop online for the office supplies for your department?

### Internet and E-mail Use

Internet use is for business purposes only. No personal e-mails, instant messaging/chatting, personal online shopping, gambling, or accessing social networking sites. Employees who violate this policy face disciplinary action, including possible termination.

A. ○ No, employees cannot use the Internet at all.
B. ○ No, online shopping is never allowed.
C. ○ Yes, only with a supervisor's approval.
D. ○ Yes, because the supplies are for the company.

**4.** How do you know how much your bonus will be?

---

### Quattro Staffing Employee Bonus Form

Name: _____     Employee ID #: _____

Number of hours worked since January 1, 2012: _____

Initial date of employment: _____

Bonus: ☐ $500   ☐ $650

- To be eligible for a bonus, you must have been employed by Quattro Staffing on January 1, 2012.

- If you worked between 1,600 and 1,699 hours in the past year, you will receive $500.

- If you worked 1,700 hours or more in the past year, you will receive $650.

---

| A. | ○ | The bonus is based only on the initial date of employment. |
| B. | ○ | The bonus is based only on the number of hours worked in the past year. |
| C. | ○ | The bonus is based on initial employment date and number of hours worked. |
| D. | ○ | Quattro Staffing gives the same bonus to all of its employees. |

**5.** According to this chart, which plants should be kept in a very sunny location?

| Check this handy sign to help keep Harris Nursery plants in tip-top shape! | | |
| --- | --- | --- |
| **Type of Plant** | **Watering Schedule** | **Light** |
| Cacti, succulents | Once per week (warm months) Once per month (cold months) | Bright light |
| Ferns | When soil is dry | Medium light |
| Bromeliads | Once per week (warm months); 1–2 times per month (cold months) | Medium light |

| A. | ○ | Cacti and succulents |
| B. | ○ | Ferns |
| C. | ○ | Ferns and bromeliads |
| D. | ○ | Bromeliads |

For more Chapter 3 assessment questions, please visit www.mysteckvaughn.com/WORK

Check your answers on page 170.

When you analyze what you read, you go beyond a simple understanding of the individual facts to find out how ideas are related. In this chapter, you will learn to analyze workplace texts by making inferences, understanding causes and effects, comparing and contrasting, and identifying facts and opinions.

# Make Inferences

## Build on What You Know

Whether or not you are conscious of it, you make **inferences** all the time. In and out of the workplace, you combine what you know with what you see and read to create meaning. You may, for example, know that a certain facial expression means a person is worried. If you see that facial expression on a friend or co-worker, you might ask, "What's wrong?" Inferences like this are based on observation and prior knowledge. You probably make them so often you don't even notice you're doing it.

Making inferences is a valuable strategy for understanding workplace documents and your work environment. When you make an inference about a workplace document, you make a logical guess based on what you know and what you read. You "read between the lines" to understand things that aren't stated directly in the text. Doing so helps you better understand what you read and helps you succeed in the workplace. In this lesson, you'll practice strategies that will help you make inferences and better understand workplace documents.

### In Real Life    Thank You for Calling

Eva is a receptionist for an advertising company. She is responsible for answering the telephone and forwarding calls and messages to her co-workers. When she started, she received the following document.

---

#### AdWorks Telephone Policy

All employees responsible for answering telephones at AdWorks should use our standard phone greeting:

"Good morning/Good afternoon. Thank you for calling AdWorks. How may I assist you?"

---

 **Discuss the following questions with a classmate. Share your ideas with the class.**

1. What is the main idea of this document?

2. Why might a company use a standard phone greeting?

3. What information helped you make these inferences?

# Read Between the Lines

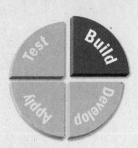

In Lesson 7, you learned strategies to locate the main idea and supporting details in a workplace document. You can use similar strategies to help you make inferences. Along with locating details, you should also think about what you already know to figure out things that are not said directly.

When you make an inference, or "read between the lines," you put what is presented in the text with what you already know to make a logical guess about the text's underlying meaning. One way to do this is to answer questions about the text by combining details from the document with your own background knowledge. The following Question-to-Inference organizer will help you make inferences using this strategy.

---

**Question:** Ask a question about the text.

| **What the document says:** Include details from the text that relate to the question. | **What I know:** Think about something you already know that is related to the details. |
|---|---|

**My answer to the question—What I infer:**
Make an inference and answer the question.

---

**Workplace Tip**

To make an inference about a workplace document, you should:

- Ask questions about the text
- Use what you know, as well as details from the text, to help you answer the questions

You may have several comments for the two middle boxes. However, your comments should build to just one inference that answers the question.

 **Look at the following document. Use the Question-to-Inference organizer to help you answer the question. Share your ideas with the class.**

---

All plumbers and assistants at R&J Plumbing are invited to sign up for a training session. Please sign up soon, as space is limited.

**Basic Procedures—Mondays, 8:00 A.M.**
Here you will learn basic skills and procedures to assist plumbers on the job. You will leave knowing the basics necessary to succeed.

**Advanced Procedures—Tuesdays, 8:00 A.M.**
Learn to read building plans, blueprints, and building codes to increase efficiency and productivity. Participants will also learn managerial skills.

---

**Question:** Which employees should take *Basic Procedures*?

| **What the document says:** *basic skills and procedures; leave knowing the basics necessary to succeed* | **What I know:** *When people start a new job, they need to learn basic skills.* |
|---|---|

**My answer to the question—What I infer:**
*Employees with little or no experience in plumbing should take this class.*

---

4. Which employees should take *Advanced Procedures*? Use the Question-to-Inference strategy to help you make an inference.

# Develop Your Skills

As you complete the activities in this lesson, use details in the text and what you already know to help you better understand workplace documents.

## Make Inferences About Workplace Documents

Remember to use the Question-to-Inference strategy you learned to help you make inferences.

 **Read the e-mail and answer the following question.**

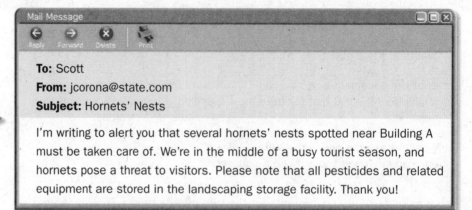

> **Mail Message**
>
> Reply   Forward   Delete   Print
>
> **To:** Scott
> **From:** jcorona@state.com
> **Subject:** Hornets' Nests
>
> I'm writing to alert you that several hornets' nests spotted near Building A must be taken care of. We're in the middle of a busy tourist season, and hornets pose a threat to visitors. Please note that all pesticides and related equipment are stored in the landscaping storage facility. Thank you!

> **Workplace Tip**
>
> Workplace documents don't always instruct. Use information in a document, along with what you know about your job responsibilities, to help you determine what action is needed.

1. What action should Scott take based on this e-mail?

## Make Inferences About Charts and Graphs

Like paragraphs in a document, charts and graphs present information. Use the same strategies for making inferences about charts and graphs.

**Review the graph and discuss the following questions with a classmate.**

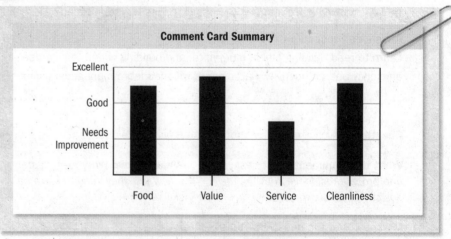

Comment Card Summary

2. Based on the graph, what does the restaurant need to improve?

3. Which kinds of employees need to improve their performance?

# Additional Tips for Making Inferences

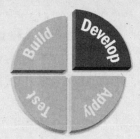

You have learned that a Question-to-Inference strategy can be helpful in organizing your thoughts as you make an inference. You can also use the following sentence starters to activate your prior knowledge when reading and making decisions in the workplace.

- *I think that . . .*
- *My guess is . . .*
- *I predict that . . .*
- *My conclusion is . . .*

 **Read the memo and answer the questions that follow.**

**To:** All Supermarket Employees
**From:** Management
**Date:** 07/09/2012
**RE:** Spinach Recall

This memo is to inform you that the state has issued a recall on certain spinach products produced by Donaldson Produce. The spinach could be contaminated. It should not be eaten or sold, and should be disposed of as soon as possible.

The recalled lots were distributed between 07/02 and 07/07. They have "Best if Used By" dates between July 13 and July 18. Thank you in advance for acting quickly to resolve this problem!

4. What action should supermarket employees take?

5. If an employee finds a spinach lot with a "Best if Used By" date of July 16, what should he or she do?

6. How should an employee respond if a concerned customer asks whether the spinach on the produce shelves is safe?

## GOT IT? | Use strategies to help you make inferences about workplace documents.

- Answer questions about a text by combining information in the text with what you already know.

- Use the Question-to-Inference strategy to help you organize your thoughts and make inferences.

- Use sentence starters such as "*I think that . . .*" to activate prior knowledge.

# Apply Your Knowledge

Use the strategies you've learned to make inferences based on each workplace document below.

**Read each of the following scenarios and its accompanying document. Select the correct response for each question.**

1. Les works for a rental car company. One of his responsibilities is inspecting cars that customers return. He receives the following memo.

> **To:** Employees
>
> **From:** Management
>
> **RE:** New Policy
>
> This memo is to inform you of a new check-in policy that has gone into effect. Customers returning rental cars are now required to sign a waiver acknowledging that Roadster Rentals is not responsible for personal items left behind in cars. Please help customers check for personal items when they return a car.

**What should Les do if he finds an MP3 player while helping check a car?**

**A.** Ask the customer to sign the waiver form.

**B.** Explain that Roadster Rentals is not responsible for the MP3 player.

**C.** Remind the customer to collect the MP3 player and other personal items.

**D.** Turn in the MP3 player at the company's front desk.

2. Why might Roadster Rentals have updated its check-in policy?

3. Gabriel works at a warehouse. One of his responsibilities is helping load and unload shipping trucks. The following sign is posted in the warehouse.

> ### Safe Loading and Unloading Practices
>
> - Wear steel-toed boots and a weight-lifting belt when loading or unloading.
> - Lift with your legs, not with your back.
> - Use a dolly or ask for help whenever necessary.
> - Maintain a clean, safe work environment.

**What should Gabriel do if he must move an object that is too heavy for him?**

**A.** Adjust his weight-lifting belt

**B.** Use a dolly or ask for help

**C.** Leave the object for somebody stronger to lift

**D.** Use his legs as he lifts instead of his back

**4.** You are training to become an auto mechanic. One of your responsibilities is helping the lead mechanic perform state inspections on automobiles. The lead mechanic prepared a document to help you perform your job.

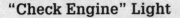

### "Check Engine" Light

Is the "Check Engine" light on when the vehicle is running? When this light is on, it means that the vehicle will require service before passing inspection. After paying for a vehicle inspection, a customer whose cars fails will have 30 days to service the vehicle and return for a free follow-up inspection.

**Based on the document, what should you tell a customer if the car's "Check Engine" light is on?**

**A.** That he or she should have the car repaired and return within 30 days

**B.** That the car will pass inspection after 30 days

**C.** That he or she will need to pay for an additional inspection

**D.** That the inspection is free because the car failed

## In Real Life   Put Your Skills to Work!

You work at a travel agency, and one of your jobs is to research travel destinations. When airline prices are high, business suffers. When airline prices are low, business is very good. Currently, airline prices for international flights are at an all-time low. Your boss would like you to create a document that lets customers know about exciting vacation destinations. What should you include in your document?

 **Think about the problem you are facing and put your skills to work! Which destinations would you include? Explain your answers.**

## Think About It!

**How can making inferences help you in your workplace?**

When you make an inference, you "read between the lines" and find the underlying meaning that may not be stated directly. Using the Question-to-Inference organizer and other strategies will help you use your prior knowledge to make inferences. This will help you understand the meaning behind many workplace documents.

# Test Your WRC Skills

**Understanding workplace documents requires a variety of reading skills. Read the following scenarios and review each document. Select the answer you think best responds to the question.**

1. You work at a popular bakery and coffee shop. Your supervisors have asked customers to complete surveys indicating what they think needs the most improvement at the bakery. Based on the following survey results, how can you help?

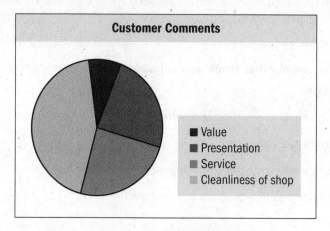

**Customer Comments**

■ Value
■ Presentation
■ Service
■ Cleanliness of shop

| | | |
|---|---|---|
| **A.** | ○ | Request that prices be dropped on baked goods. |
| **B.** | ○ | Improve how the baked goods look. |
| **C.** | ○ | Serve customers more quickly. |
| **D.** | ○ | Spend more time cleaning the bakery. |

2. You work as an animal caretaker, and one of your responsibilities is feeding and medicating animals. Which animals will need the most care?

| Pet Name | Feeding Times | Medication* |
|---|---|---|
| Max | 9:00 A.M./3:00 P.M. | None |
| Tallulah | 9:00 A.M./3:00 P.M. | None |
| Spot | 9:00 A.M./3:00 P.M. | 9:00 A.M./4:00 P.M. |
| Daisy | 9:00 A.M./3:00 P.M. | 9:00 A.M./4:00 P.M. |

*Animals needing medication may require more time than is outlined on the schedule.

| | | |
|---|---|---|
| **A.** | ○ | Spot and Daisy |
| **B.** | ○ | Max and Tallulah |
| **C.** | ○ | Tallulah and Spot |
| **D.** | ○ | All of the animals will require the same amount of care. |

**3.** According to this sign, what should employees do?

**A Green Office Starts With You!**

REDUCE RECYCLE REUSE

| A. | ○ | Help paint the office green. |
| B. | ○ | Start a recycling program at work. |
| C. | ○ | Cut down on waste and recycle whenever possible. |
| D. | ○ | Report any employees that are being wasteful. |

**4.** According to the following e-mail message, how did Rachel earn her promotion?

> We are excited to announce that Rachel Sanchez has been promoted to the position of Assistant Manager. Rachel started as a customer service representative in the hardware department over three years ago. We truly appreciate her continued hard work and eagerness to learn and take on more responsibility. As an assistant manager, Rachel will lead and train new customer service representatives. Please join us in congratulating her.

| A. | ○ | By passing a customer service representative management test |
| B. | ○ | By working at the company for more than three years |
| C. | ○ | By helping to train her fellow customer service representatives |
| D. | ○ | By working hard and being eager to learn and take on more responsibility |

**5.** According to the document, which employees should take *Managing Workflow*?

> All carpenters are invited to participate in the following training programs:
>
> **Knowing the Basics—Wednesdays, 8:00 A.M.**
>
> Learn about the various tools and skills you will need to succeed on the job.
>
> **Managing Workflow—Mondays, 8:00 A.M.**
>
> Learn to maintain job records and schedule work crews. Also learn skills for reading blueprints and diagrams to draw up accurate construction plans.

| A. | ○ | New employees who would rather work as managers than carpenters |
| B. | ○ | Employees who have just completed *Knowing the Basics* |
| C. | ○ | Experienced employees who wish to learn more about managing |
| D. | ○ | Employees with no construction experience |

Check your
answers on
page 170.

# Identify Cause and Effect

## Essential Tasks

**Analyze and interpret meaning** of simple work-related texts

## Build on What You Know

Have you ever been late for lunch with a friend? What was the **cause**? Perhaps you got lost or forgot what time you were supposed to meet. What was an **effect**? Your friend may have been annoyed with you. Or perhaps you decided that you would try harder to be on time next time.

Cause-and-effect relationships influence many parts of your life, including work. Your actions will always have causes and effects. The rules of your workplace and other decisions that are made also have causes and effects. Recognizing causes and effects in workplace documents can help you understand your job responsibilities, as well as the reasons behind them. This lesson will help you understand cause-and-effect relationships and identify them in the texts you read on the job.

### In Real Life    Not a Bright Idea

Mai, a nursery worker at Gray's Greenhouse, is rushing to complete her end-of-shift tasks so that she can leave for a doctor's appointment. She quickly glances at the instructions below, but she misses the note about not placing these flowers in direct sunlight. When she finishes watering and feeding the flowers, Mai places them in a sunny spot, locks up the nursery, and hurries out to catch her bus.

---

**AFRICAN VIOLET**

*(Saintpaulia ionantha)*

**Care Instructions:** Store at temperatures above 60°F. Keep soil slightly moist at all times. Water with warm water so that the leaves do not spot. Feed with a water-soluble fertilizer.

*Note:* Do not leave flowers in direct sunlight because their leaves will burn.

---

 **Discuss the following questions with a classmate. Share your ideas with the class.**

1. Why do you think Mai missed some of the directions?

2. What might happen to the flowers?

3. What other consequences might Mai's actions have?

**Teacher Reminder**
Review the teacher lesson at
www.mysteckvaughn.com/WORK

**120** Reading

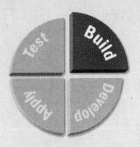

# What Is Cause and Effect?

A cause is why something happens, and an effect is what happens as a result. Sometimes cause-and-effect relationships in workplace documents are easy to spot. But sometimes these important relationships are not directly stated. In Lesson 11, you learned that you make inferences by putting the information you read together with what you already know to find the underlying meaning. Making inferences can help you identify causes and effects that are not directly stated.

Suppose you are leaving an unfamiliar building after making a delivery. You see this sign. Though the sign does not say, "Opening this door will cause an alarm to go off," you can infer that if you push the door open, the effect will be that an alarm will sound.

# Cause and Effect in Workplace Documents

There are several reasons why employers create workplace documents that explain causes and effects. These documents:

- Keep you and others safe.

- Inform you of rules and consequences.

- Help you succeed.

Keeping the above purposes in mind can help you identify causes and effects in any type of workplace document you encounter. For example, imagine you see a "Caution: Do Not Block Loading Dock" sign with an image of somebody tripping over a box. Take a minute to think about the reasons the sign is posted. You should recognize that the sign's purpose is to keep to you safe—if you block the loading dock (cause), somebody could get hurt (effect).

**Read the following scenarios and discuss the purpose of the documents. Then discuss causes and effects that the documents might describe.**

4. Your supervisor thinks you should pursue a promotion in the company. She gives you a document that shows how you can get the job.

5. You see a sign posted above the meat slicer, warning you to unplug the machine before cleaning it.

6. You are asked to review an employee policy that explains what time you are expected to arrive and what will happen if you do not show up on time.

7. You read a poster explaining how to prevent food contamination while preparing meal orders.

# Develop Your Skills

You now know what cause-and-effect relationships are and some reasons why they may be found in workplace documents. Below are some useful techniques to help you identify causes and effects in texts you might see on the job.

## Ask Questions

Ask questions about the workplace documents you read to identify cause and effect. Here are some example questions.

| Cause Questions | Effect Questions |
|---|---|
| · How did this happen? | · What will happen as a result? |
| · What is the reason for this? | · What are the consequences? |
| · Why will this occur? | · What is the outcome? |
| · Why should I do this? | · How will this affect me? |

Depending on what you are reading, some questions might be more helpful than others. If a certain question does not help you find an answer, try asking a different one. You might find that there is more than one answer to your question. Sometimes there are several causes of a single effect, or several effects from a single cause.

 **Look at the following document. Identify whether the questions below require you to find the cause or the effect.**

---

### New Supply Ordering Procedure

In order to cut back on spending, our office will be implementing a new supply ordering procedure. All employees requesting supplies will have to submit a supply order request form to their supervisors. All supervisors will then give the forms to the office manager. The office manager will review the forms to be certain that no duplicate requests are made. This will prevent departments from ordering supplies that have already been purchased by another department.

---

1. What is the reason for the new supply ordering procedure?

2. What will the outcome of the new procedure be on the company's budget?

3. How will the new procedure affect the employees?

4. Why will the office manager review the supply order request forms?

# Signal Words

Remember that signal words are words that give you clues. In Lesson 5, you learned about signal words that show sequence. There are also signal words that show cause and effect. Look for the following words and phrases to identify cause-and-effect relationships in workplace documents:

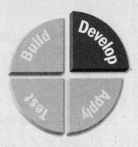

| Cause-and-Effect Signal Words | | | |
|---|---|---|---|
| as a result | consequently | so that | if . . . then |
| because | due to | in order that | thus |
| since | as a consequence | for this reason | hence |
| so | accordingly | therefore | on account of |

 **Read the following document and answer the questions.**

---

### Employee Action Report

**Employee:** Erin O'Brian
**Supervisor:** Abeeku Badu
☑ Employee Status Change
❑ Disciplinary Warning

Supervisor Comments: Due to superior performance as a product promoter, Ms. O'Brian is being promoted to Product Promoter Trainer. Her new responsibilities will include recruiting and training new product promoters. Also, because Ms. O'Brian showed great ability to organize, she will be in charge of setting up the promotional booths. Ms. O'Brian is a wonderful employee, and I am confident she will succeed in her new role.

Employee Signature _____ Date _____
Supervisor Signature _____ Date _____

---

5. What signal words or phrases can you find in the document?

6. How do the signal words or phrases help you understand the cause-and-effect relationships in the document?

## GOT IT?  To identify cause and effect:

- Think about the purpose of the document.
- Remember that there can be several causes or several effects.
- Ask questions.
- Look for signal words.

**Answer Key**

1. Cause (To cut back on spending)
2. Effect (The company will save money)
3. Effect (They will need to change the way they order supplies.)
4. Cause (To prevent duplicate orders)
5. *Due to*, *because*
6. The phrase *due to* introduces the cause of Ms. O'Brian's promotion (her superior performance). *Because* introduces the reason why Ms. O'Brian will now be in charge of setting up the promotional booths (her ability to organize).

**To-Do List**

Remember to follow these steps when applying your knowledge:

❏ **Think about the purpose of the document.**

❏ **Remember that there can be several causes or effects.**

❏ **Ask questions.**

❏ **Look for signal words.**

# Apply Your Knowledge

Look for cause and effect in workplace documents to stay safe, learn rules and consequences, and succeed at your job. Asking questions and locating signal words are two techniques that can help you identify cause and effect in workplace documents.

**Read each of the following scenarios and interpret its accompanying document. Select the correct response for each question.**

1. Lauren works as a home care aide for the elderly. Her daily tasks include helping patients with basic hygiene, cooking, and completing light housekeeping. Lauren is reviewing instructions in a new patient's file. She reads the following section.

> **ALLERGIES:** Mr. Emerson has no drug allergies. He does have several severe food allergies, including all wheat products. Due to Mr. Emerson's strict dietary restrictions, a list of appropriate meals and how to prepare them has been provided. See attached page.

**Based on the instructions, why is a list of meals provided?**

**A.** Lauren might get hungry while caring for Mr. Emerson.

**B.** Mr. Emerson has many food restrictions.

**C.** Mr. Emerson likes to eat meals containing wheat.

**D.** Lauren does not know how to cook.

2. What effect might result if Lauren does not follow the instructions?

3. You are interviewing for a job at a local factory. You know that there are a lot of complicated machines, and you express your concerns about work-related injuries to the factory manager. He shows you the following graph.

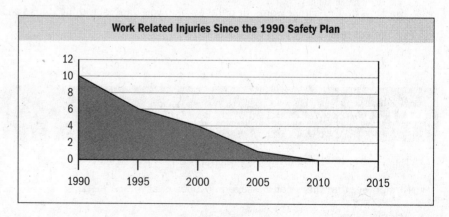

**Work Related Injuries Since the 1990 Safety Plan**

**Based on the graph, what is the result of the 1990 Safety Plan?**

**A.** The number of work-related injuries stayed the same.

**B.** The number of work-related injuries increased.

**C.** The number of work-related injuries decreased.

**D.** The number of work-related injuries only affected certain employees.

4. The weather forecaster has predicted that a huge blizzard will come through your area in the late afternoon. You receive the following e-mail.

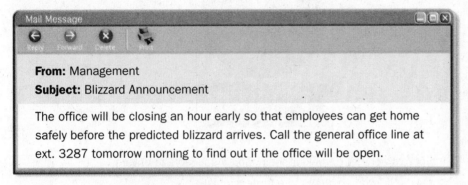

Mail Message

Reply  Forward  Delete  Print

**From:** Management

**Subject:** Blizzard Announcement

The office will be closing an hour early so that employees can get home safely before the predicted blizzard arrives. Call the general office line at ext. 3287 tomorrow morning to find out if the office will be open.

**How will the early closing affect you?**

**A.** You need to leave early from work.

**B.** You will have to drive home in the blizzard.

**C.** You will not have to go to work tomorrow.

**D.** You will have two days off from work.

## In Real Life    Put Your Skills to Work!

You work in the shipping department at a computer company. Several addresses on order forms have been typed incorrectly, which causes a number of shipments to be returned. You will write a memo reminding employees to be careful when inputting information in order forms.

 **Think about the problem you are facing and put your skills to work! What causes and effects would you include?**

> **Workplace Tip**
>
> When making your memo, think about:
> • Why you are writing
> • Signal words you could include
> • The effect you hope to achieve

### Think About It!

**How can understanding cause and effect in workplace documents help you?**

Identifying cause and effect in workplace documents will help you understand your job responsibilities, as well as the reasons behind them. This strategy can help you succeed at your job.

**Answer Key**

**1.** B

**2.** Mr. Emerson could get very sick.

**3.** C

**4.** A

# Test Your WRC Skills

**Identifying cause and effect in workplace documents can help you understand the reasons and results of actions in the workplace. Read the following scenarios and review each document. Select the answer you think best responds to the question.**

**1.** What is the **MOST** likely reason for posting this sign for highway maintenance workers?

High visibility clothing must be worn at this site.

| | | |
|---|---|---|
| **A.** | ○ | It protects workers by making them more noticeable to drivers. |
| **B.** | ○ | It makes the workers look more professional. |
| **C.** | ○ | It reminds workers that they are at work. |
| **D.** | ○ | It keeps drivers from driving in construction areas. |

**2.** According to this memo, what will happen first if an employee does **NOT** cover his or her tattoos?

> To: All Employees
>
> From: Human Resources
>
> Date: January 4, 2012
>
> Subject: Tattoo and Piercing Policy
>
> This is a reminder that all bank employees in direct contact with customers must cover all tattoos and remove all piercings (with the exception of earrings). Our bank prides itself on having high professional appearance standards and expects all employees to present a businesslike image. Employees who do not comply with this policy will receive a verbal warning from their supervisor. A written warning will be issued and placed on record if the employee still does not comply. A third warning will result in immediate disciplinary action, based on the discretion of the supervisor.

| | | |
|---|---|---|
| **A.** | ○ | The supervisor will decide the consequences based on the circumstances. |
| **B.** | ○ | The employee will receive a note instructing that the tattoo be covered. |
| **C.** | ○ | The supervisor will tell the employee to cover the tattoo. |
| **D.** | ○ | The employee will be fired immediately by his or her supervisor. |

**3.** According to this flow chart, what will happen if a clock face does **NOT** pass inspection when it is checked for quality?

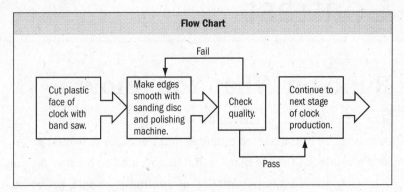

| | | |
|---|---|---|
| **A.** | ○ | It will be thrown away. |
| **B.** | ○ | It will be sent back to be smoothed. |
| **C.** | ○ | It will be sent back to be re-cut. |
| **D.** | ○ | It will continue to the next step in production. |

**4.** Based on the graph, why might your restaurant manager often ask you to work on Saturdays?

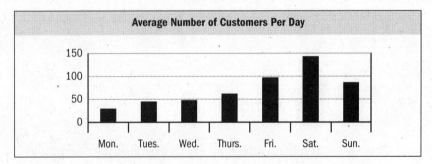

| | | |
|---|---|---|
| **A.** | ○ | Customers like the specials offered on Saturdays. |
| **B.** | ○ | The average number of customers is the least on Saturdays. |
| **C.** | ○ | Your manager usually cannot work on Saturdays. |
| **D.** | ○ | The restaurant gets the most business on Saturdays. |

**5.** According to this policy, what is the **MOST** likely reason owners must prove that their pets are healthy before boarding them at the vet?

> The safety and health of your pet is our primary concern. For this reason, we require proof that your pet is up-to-date on all vaccinations and does not have any parasites or fleas. At your request, we will gladly vaccinate or treat your pet for parasites prior to boarding.

| | | |
|---|---|---|
| **A.** | ◉ | The vet does not want to expose boarded pets to sick animals. |
| **B.** | ○ | The vet wants to make money by vaccinating and treating pets with parasites. |
| **C.** | ○ | The vet does not have time to treat more sick animals. |
| **D.** | ○ | The vet does not trust its clients to keep their pets healthy. |

Check your
answers on
page 171.

# Compare and Contrast

## Build on What You Know

Have you ever tried to choose between two cell phone plans? One plan may give you five hundred free minutes, and the other may offer seven hundred. When you look at these plans, what details are the most important to you? Which are the least important? What information might get you to choose one plan over the other?

Understanding similarities and differences is also important when reading workplace documents. When you read, you often need to **compare**, or find similarities. You also need to **contrast**, or find differences. A workplace document may compare and contrast different ideas, issues, or events. The information may appear in different forms and formats. Knowing how to compare and contrast in the context of workplace documents can help you pay attention to details, narrow down your choices, and make important decisions.

### In Real Life  Which Paint?

Tess works at a hardware store and is assigned to the painting supplies department. She needs to know which types of brushes to recommend for each customer's needs. She also needs to explain the types of paint sheens that are best for different indoor and outdoor surfaces. One day a customer in the paint aisle is looking at this chart:

| Indoor Paints | | Outdoor Paints | |
|---|---|---|---|
| Sheens: | | Sheens: | |
| • flat | • satin | • flat | |
| • matte | • semi-gloss | • semi-gloss | |
| • eggshell | • high-gloss | • high-gloss | |

Tess asks the customer questions about his painting project so that she can help him select the proper sheen from the chart.

 **Discuss the following questions. Share your ideas with the class.**

1. What questions might Tess ask the customer?

2. Is it important that Tess know details about each type of paint sheen? Why or why not?

3. How could Tess's knowledge help the customer make a decision?

**Teacher Reminder**
Review the teacher lesson at
www.mysteckvaughn.com/WORK

**128** Reading

# Digging Deeper

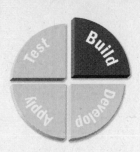

In Lesson 11, you learned that sometimes you need to find information in a document that is not obvious or stated directly. You learned how to put together what you already know and what you read. You also discovered that when important details seem unclear or hidden, you may need to make inferences based on the limited information that the document provides.

Like making inferences, understanding how ideas in a document are alike or different often requires that you look beyond what may be obvious or clearly stated. Here are some key words to help you understand the language used to describe information in workplace texts:

| Compare | To focus on the ways two or more things are the *same* |
| Similarity | A feature that people, things, or ideas have in common |
| Contrast | To focus on the ways two or more things are *different* |
| Difference | A feature that distinguishes people, things, or ideas |

 **Think of two places where you have lived, and answer the questions.**

**4.** What are the differences between these places?

**5.** Are there any similarities between the two places?

One useful way to organize and visualize similarities and differences is to use a Venn diagram. This type of organizer can help you understand how two things are different, as well as the similarities they may share.

 **Look at the Venn diagram below, which compares and contrasts the details of two health care plans. Then answer the questions that follow.**

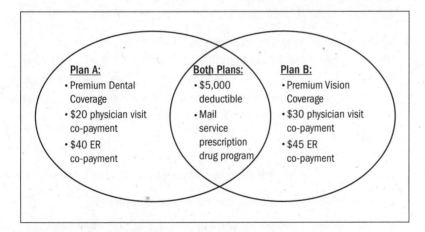

**6.** How is Plan A different from Plan B?

**7.** How are the health care plans alike?

**8.** When might you use a Venn diagram to organize your ideas?

# Develop Your Skills

Locating similarities and differences can help you identify a document's important details. The tools below can help you find these details.

## Signal Words and Phrases

You have learned some signal words that show sequence and other signal words that help you identify causes and effects. There are also signal words that help you locate similarities and differences in a document. Signal words used to compare tell you how two or more things are alike. Signal words used to contrast provide clues about how things are different.

| Signal Words and Phrases | |
|---|---|
| **To Compare:** | **To Contrast:** |
| same | different |
| similarly | however |
| both | but |
| as well | although |
| like/alike | whereas |
| also | on the other hand |
| too | instead of |

 **Read the memo. Then use the signal words chart to help you answer the questions that follow.**

### MEMO

**To:** All Customer Service Representatives

**From:** Managers at Quality Vacuums, Inc.

**RE:** The New 300Z Vacuum Is Here!

Tomorrow we will begin selling our new 300Z model vacuum. This is a newer version of our 200Z. Both the 200Z and 300Z are durable and have great suction, but the new model is different because it is bagless. The older model is heavy, whereas the new model weighs only 7 pounds. The 200Z and 300Z come with the same filtering system. However, the 300Z's filter is easier to clean.

1. What signal words are used to compare and contrast information?

2. What two things are being compared and contrasted?

3. Why would the managers at Quality Vacuums, Inc., send this memo to their customer service representatives?

**Create a Venn diagram. Fill in the diagram with information comparing the 200Z and 300Z vacuums. Discuss your diagram with a classmate.**

4. What features do both vacuum models have in common?

# Compare and Contrast Using Graphics

Although they may not use signal words and phrases, you can find important comparisons in workplace charts and graphs. Identifying the similarities and differences shown in a chart or graph can help you understand the information and why it is being presented.

 **Look at this line graph from a gym's sales team meeting. The gym members pay for each class, and the sales team must analyze which classes are making the most and the least money.**

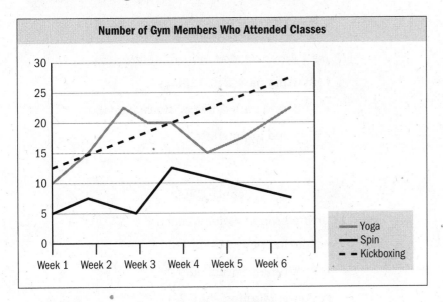

**Number of Gym Members Who Attended Classes**

Legend:
— Yoga
— Spin
- - - Kickboxing

5. What time period is covered in the graph?

6. What information is being compared in the graph?

7. Which type of class has the highest overall attendance?

8. How many gym members went to yoga classes in Week 1?

 **Discuss how the sales team might use the information in the graph.**

9. How could salespeople encourage more gym members to attend spin classes?

10. How might the information in the graph affect the gym's schedule?

---

**GOT IT?**

**Comparing and contrasting is a useful strategy that can help you understand workplace documents. When you compare and contrast:**

- Look for signal words that may help you identify similarities and differences.
- Identify important comparisons in charts and graphs.
- Use the similarities and differences to make decisions or inferences.

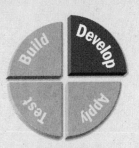

**Answer Key**

1. The signal words are: *both, but, different, whereas, same,* and *however.*

2. The old 200Z and new 300Z vacuum models

3. Possible answer: Managers would send this memo so that the customer service representatives can answer customers' questions about the vacuums.

4. Both vacuums are durable, have great suction, and have a filtering system.

5. Six weeks

6. The graph compares the number of gym members who attended yoga, spin, and kickboxing classes.

7. Kickboxing

8. 10

9. Possible answer: The sales team could give each member a coupon for one free spin class.

10. Possible answer: The gym may change the schedule to offer more yoga classes and fewer spin classes.

# Apply Your Knowledge

Comparing and contrasting requires that you look at a document's details to find important similarities and differences.

**Read each of the following scenarios and its accompanying documents. Select the correct response for each question.**

**1.** You finished your training, and you are now a certified nurse's aide. You want to find a full-time position and you see the following job postings.

<u>City Hospital</u>

*Nurse's Aides Needed Immediately!*

- **Starting pay:  $10–12/hour**
- **Full- and part-time positions available**
- **Day and night shifts**

<u>County Clinic</u>

*1 Certified Nurse's Aide Needed.*

- **Starting pay:  $13–15/hour**
- **Part-time position only**
- **Hours: Morning shift, 7–11**

**Based on the information in the two job postings:**

**A.** City Hospital offers a higher starting pay rate than County Clinic.

**B.** City Hospital has more than one job opening.

**C.** The job at County Clinic offers full-time positions.

**D.** The job at County Clinic is too far away.

**2.** Based on question 1, why is the City Hospital position a better option for you?

**3.** Mr. Lau is an assistant manager at Super Electronics. Mr. Lau must encourage the employees in his department to get customers to sign up for a Super Electronics Rewards Card. Each week he figures out which of his employees signed up the most customers for a rewards card.

| Rewards Card Sign-ups | | | | | | | |
|---|---|---|---|---|---|---|---|
| | Mon. | Tues. | Wed. | Thurs. | Fri. | Sat. | Sun. | Total |
| Miguel | 5 | 1 | 5 | OFF | 5 | 2 | 6 | **24** |
| Jasmine | OFF | 5 | 6 | 5 | 1 | 4 | 5 | **26** |
| Lee | 1 | OFF | 5 | 5 | 7 | 5 | 1 | **24** |
| Jamie | 1 | 3 | 5 | 5 | OFF | 5 | 4 | **23** |

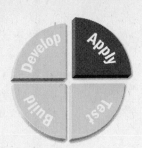

**Based on the information in the chart, this week Lee:**

A. Signed up the fewest customers

B. Signed up the most customers

C. Signed up more customers than Miguel

D. Signed up fewer customers than Jasmine

4. Who signed up the most customers on Wednesday?

A. Miguel

B. Jasmine

C. Lee

D. Jamie

## In Real Life  Put Your Skills to Work!

All employees at the store where you work want to convince the store owners to purchase new cash registers and scanning devices. At today's staff meeting, the employees are discussing how a new checkout system could save time when the store gets busy. Several employees voice various complaints about the old, outdated registers and scanners. Your manager wants to send a request to the store owners about the need for an updated checkout system. She asks you and your co-workers to prepare a document that explains why the new checkout system would be better than the old one.

 **Think about the problem you are facing and put your skills to work! What kinds of details would you include in the document? How would you organize this information? Explain your ideas.**

**Workplace Tip**

When you create your document, how would you present the similarities and differences between the two checkout systems?

## Think About It!

**When might you need to compare and contrast information at work?**

Comparing and contrasting is a useful strategy that can help you identify and connect the important details in a document. You may encounter workplace documents that present similarities and differences in many different ways and use various formats. Understanding how to compare and contrast the information can help you make good decisions and inferences on the job.

**Answer Key**

**1.** B

**2.** Possible answer: City Hospital is a better option because you are looking for a full-time position. County Clinic's posting says it has only one part-time position.

**3.** D

**4.** B

# Test Your WRC Skills

Comparing and contrasting requires that you identify important details in texts. Read the following scenarios and review each document. Select the answer you think best responds to the question.

1. Someone who wants to get a job fixing car air conditioners should enroll in which of Community College's programs?

| Current Programs at Community College | | |
|---|---|---|
| **Program Title** | **Brief Overview** | **Course Offerings** |
| **Commercial Electrician** | Learn about high voltage installations in industrial buildings. | Courses offered in the spring and fall |
| **Residential Electrician** | Learn about low voltage installations in homes. | Courses offered in the spring, summer, and fall |
| **HVAC Technician** | Learn heating, ventilation, and air conditioning systems for automobiles, buildings, and homes. | Courses offered in the spring and fall |
| **Electrical Engineer/Aviation** | Learn electronic systems for planes. | Courses offered in the fall only |

A. ○ Commercial Electrician
B. ○ Residential Electrician
C. ○ HVAC Technician
D. ○ Electrical Engineer/Aviation

2. Employees at Snowy Lodge should recommend which trail for customers who have never skied before?

> **Snowy Lodge Trail Guide**
>
> **Sky Mountain I:** This slope is for experienced skiers only. There is some dangerous terrain.
>
> **Sky Mountain II:** Advanced skiers only. Half-pipe open on weekends only.
>
> **Sun Mountain:** This is a beginner slope. People of all ages and abilities welcome.
>
> **Mountain Peak:** Intermediate slope with moderate terrain. No half-pipe.

A. ○ Sky Mountain I
B. ○ Sky Mountain II
C. ○ Sun Mountain
D. ○ Mountain Peak

**3.** According to this e-mail, which of ABC's teams have the **LONGEST** training?

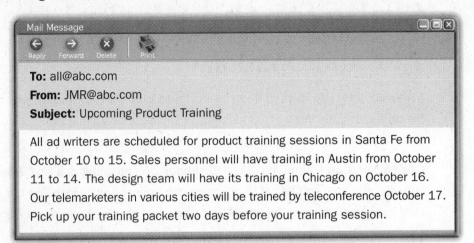

Mail Message

Reply   Forward   Delete   Print

**To:** all@abc.com

**From:** JMR@abc.com

**Subject:** Upcoming Product Training

All ad writers are scheduled for product training sessions in Santa Fe from October 10 to 15. Sales personnel will have training in Austin from October 11 to 14. The design team will have its training in Chicago on October 16. Our telemarketers in various cities will be trained by teleconference October 17. Pick up your training packet two days before your training session.

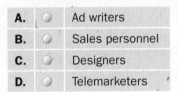

| A. | ○ | Ad writers |
| B. | ○ | Sales personnel |
| C. | ○ | Designers |
| D. | ○ | Telemarketers |

**4.** Which members of this EMT team can perform the **HIGHEST** level of emergency care?

| **EMT 1:** | **EMT 2:** |
| --- | --- |
| · Performs basic emergency care | · Performs basic emergency care |
| · May not use defibrillator | · May use defibrillator |
| · May not give oral and intravenous drugs | · May not give oral and intravenous drugs |
| **EMT 3:** | **EMT 4:** |
| · May use defibrillator | · May use defibrillator |
| · May administer fluids intravenously | · May give oral and intravenous drugs |
| · May not give oral and intravenous drugs | · May perform all EMT 1, 2, and 3 duties |

| A. | ○ | EMT 1 |
| B. | ○ | EMT 2 |
| C. | ○ | EMT 3 |
| D. | ○ | EMT 4 |

**5.** Based on the memo below, sales in which department have increased the **MOST**?

**MEMO**

**To:** All Store Employees

**From:** Ms. Etto

**RE:** Sales in our Kids' Departments

I want to let you know about our recent sales numbers. Sales of girls' outerwear have gone up 7%, and boys' outerwear sales have gone up 10%. Sales in the boys' shoe department rose 6%, but sales in the girls' shoe department fell 2%.

| A. | ○ | Girls' outerwear |
| B. | ○ | Boys' outerwear |
| C. | ○ | Girls' shoes |
| D. | ○ | Boys' shoes |

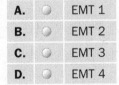

Check your answers on page 171.

# Skills for the Workplace

## Fact and Opinion

In this chapter, you learned to go beyond words on the page and think about the underlying meaning of a document. You can make an inference, think about cause and effect, or compare and contrast.

**Critical reading** is thinking about the underlying meaning of a text. Reading critically can help you better understand documents and succeed on the job. Differentiating between **facts** and **opinions** will also help you read critically.

**Facts** are statements that can be proven. For example:

- Sales are down 6 percent this quarter.
- Yolanda worked 50 hours this week.
- Employees can wear white or black shirts with their uniforms.

**Opinions** are statements that express what someone feels or believes. They cannot be proven. The following statements are opinions:

- Sales this quarter are too low.
- Yolanda should not work so hard.
- The white shirts look better than the black shirts.

As you read, ask yourself the following questions:

- Could this information be proven to be true? *(fact)*
- Does this statement express what someone believes? *(opinion)*
- Does this statement contain opinion signal words, such as *think, believe, best, worst, too _____, not _____ enough,* or *should? (opinion)*
- Could you disagree with this statement? *(opinion)*

## Workplace Scenario

Read each statement below. Is it a fact or an opinion?

- These uniforms are ugly and out of style. *Opinion: It expresses a feeling or belief about the uniforms.*
- Our uniforms haven't changed in ten years. *Fact: It can be proven.*
- It would be better if we didn't have to wear uniforms. *Opinion: It cannot be proven.*
- Only 20 percent of managers in this company are women. *Fact: You can prove it by counting all the men and women who are managers.*
- Our company should have more female managers. *Opinion: It expresses a belief and cannot be proven.*

## Workplace Practice

Consider the following facts:

- You have a co-worker named Jack.

- Jack has been late four out of five days this week.

- Jack does not always follow the safety procedures and often asks others to do his work for him.

Use the facts and the questions below to form two opinions about Jack.

- Is Jack a good worker? *No. Jack does not come to work on time, follow the rules, or complete his own work. These facts support the opinion that Jack is not a good worker.*

- Should Jack be considered for the next promotion in your group? *No. The listed facts and the opinion that Jack is not a good worker both support the opinion that Jack should not be promoted.*

The example above shows that facts can be used to support opinions. Imagine that your supervisor asked you whether you thought Jack should be promoted. You could give your opinion, but that alone may not persuade your supervisor. Using facts to support your opinions will help others see that your opinion is based on more than just personal likes and dislikes.

When you read facts, think about what opinions the facts support. When you read opinions, ask yourself, *What are the facts that support this opinion? Would I draw the same opinion from these facts?* Thinking critically about facts and opinions can help you understand the decisions others make. It can also help you make good decisions and succeed on the job.

### It's Your Turn!

1. Your company requires you to purchase your uniform from one store, even though the same clothing is available elsewhere. In your opinion, the clothing at that store is overpriced. What facts might you give to support this opinion?

2. How might you convince management to allow employees to purchase uniforms from another store?

3. Your boss tells you she feels strongly that employees should be on time for all meetings. How might understanding this opinion help you on the job?

4. A few of your co-workers are always complaining about the job. One day they say, "We should go on strike." How will you decide whether you agree or disagree with their opinion?

> **Workplace Tip**
>
> Some opinions are more objective than others and, thus, can support facts. When presented with an opinion, try to decide whether that opinion could objectively support a fact.

*It's Your Turn!* **Answer Key**

**1.** You could provide prices from several stores, showing the difference in price.

**2.** You could express your opinion and support it with facts.

**3.** Even though you may not agree with your boss's opinion, understanding it can help you meet your boss's expectations.

**4.** Before agreeing with your co-workers, you should make sure you understand the facts that support their opinion.

# Chapter 4 Assessment

**Select the answer you think best responds to the question.**

**1.** Which employees should enroll in the medical center's on-site day care?

> **Enroll in University Medical Center On-Site Day Care**
>
> We are proud to announce that University Medical Center now offers on-site day care as a service to its employees. Day care hours are 8:00 A.M. to 6:00 P.M. We will provide care and activities for children under age 12. Day care costs $350 per month.

- **A.** ○ Employees with young children
- **B.** ○ Employees who don't have children
- **C.** ○ Employees with children in high school
- **D.** ○ Employees who want free day care

**2.** How do large flower arrangements differ from small flower arrangements?

> **Small Flower Arrangements:** Choose a vase less than 5 inches wide at the base. Use small to medium flowers, such as carnations. Use filler and greenery.
>
> **Large Flower Arrangements:** Choose a vase at least 5 inches wide at the base. Use mainly large flowers, such as lilies. Vary the heights of the flowers. Use filler and greenery.

- **A.** ○ Large arrangements require vases less than 5 inches wide at the base.
- **B.** ○ Large arrangements do not have any filler or greenery.
- **C.** ○ Large arrangements require vases at least 5 inches wide at the base.
- **D.** ○ Large arrangements have small to medium flowers.

**3.** Manor Electronics adopted new customer service guidelines at the end of the first quarter. Based on the graph, what were the results of the new customer service guidelines?

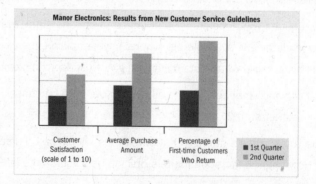

- **A.** ○ Customer satisfaction decreased, and average purchase amount increased.
- **B.** ○ The percentage of first-time customers who returned to the store decreased.
- **C.** ○ Customer satisfaction and the average purchase amount both increased.
- **D.** ○ Average purchase amount stayed the same between the first and second quarter.

**4.** How should Jared improve his job performance, according to the employee evaluation?

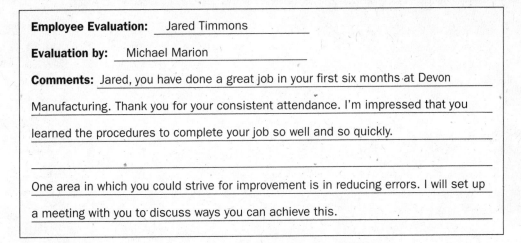

Employee Evaluation: <u>Jared Timmons</u>

Evaluation by: <u>Michael Marion</u>

Comments: <u>Jared, you have done a great job in your first six months at Devon</u>

<u>Manufacturing. Thank you for your consistent attendance. I'm impressed that you</u>

<u>learned the procedures to complete your job so well and so quickly.</u>

<u></u>

<u>One area in which you could strive for improvement is in reducing errors. I will set up</u>

<u>a meeting with you to discuss ways you can achieve this.</u>

| A. | ○ | Jared should try to get along with other employees better. |
| B. | ○ | Jared should learn ways to reduce errors. |
| C. | ○ | Jared should have better attendance. |
| D. | ○ | Jared should learn the procedures for completing his job. |

**5.** Based on the e-mail, what do you think will happen at the meeting?

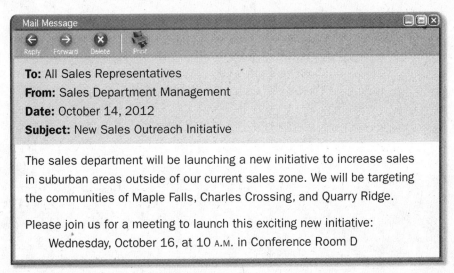

Mail Message

Reply　Forward　Delete　Print

**To:** All Sales Representatives
**From:** Sales Department Management
**Date:** October 14, 2012
**Subject:** New Sales Outreach Initiative

The sales department will be launching a new initiative to increase sales in suburban areas outside of our current sales zone. We will be targeting the communities of Maple Falls, Charles Crossing, and Quarry Ridge.

Please join us for a meeting to launch this exciting new initiative:
Wednesday, October 16, at 10 A.M. in Conference Room D

| A. | ○ | Sales department management will discuss old sales initiatives. |
| B. | ○ | Someone from Human Resources will discuss salary changes. |
| C. | ○ | Sales representatives will be assigned urban locations to target. |
| D. | ○ | Sales representatives will be assigned suburban communities to target. |

Check your answers on page 172.

 For more Chapter 4 assessment questions, please visit www.mysteckvaughn.com/WORK

CHAPTER

# 5 Integrate New Information with Prior Knowledge

Putting what you learn together with what you already know is a powerful strategy for understanding workplace texts and graphics. In this chapter, you will learn and practice this strategy by applying information to a new context, synthesizing information from multiple sources, and understanding workplace jargon.

# 14 Apply Information to a New Context

## Build on What You Know

Have you ever had to study for something? Chances are that you have—and more than once in your life. Perhaps you studied to pass a test in school or to get your driver's license. Studying is a skill that you have used over and over again to prepare for many different things. In essence, you have applied the same skill to succeed in a variety of circumstances.

At work, you may also be required to use what you already know and apply it to new contexts, or situations. Whether you are transferring skills from one workplace to another or using what you know to solve new problems at a current job, drawing on prior knowledge can help you accomplish a variety of tasks. This lesson will teach you how to use what you already know and apply it to new contexts in the workplace.

### In Real Life    At Your Service

Daria has been waiting tables for a year at a local restaurant. Her responsibilities include taking food orders, serving meals, handling payments, clearing and setting tables, and making sure customers enjoy their dining experience. The restaurant where Daria works is closing, so she decides to apply for this job as a front desk clerk at a hotel.

> **Help Wanted**
>
> **Position:** Front Desk Clerk
>
> **Description:** Looking for someone to welcome and serve hotel guests politely and efficiently. Individual will be expected to take reservations, check guests in and out, handle payments, and respond to guest requests. You must be able to stand for long periods of time and demonstrate basic computer skills.

**Discuss the following questions with a classmate. Share your ideas with the class.**

1. Why do you think Daria chose to apply for this job?

2. How can Daria use what she already knows about waiting tables to work as a front desk clerk at a hotel?

3. What other types of jobs might Daria apply for?

## Prior Knowledge

Your **prior knowledge** is everything you already know. It is often necessary to have a certain amount of prior knowledge in order to understand workplace documents and complete workplace duties. In previous lessons, you learned how to use what you already know and what you read to find meaning that isn't directly stated in a document. This chapter explores how you can use what you already know and what you read to complete new tasks or solve new problems at work.

You probably have a lot more prior knowledge about the workplace than you think. If you have ever been a customer or client, you have an idea about how certain businesses work. For example, though you may never have worked in a grocery store, you know what kinds of things you can buy there. You probably also know the store layout and some things that employees are required to do. Using this kind of prior knowledge can help you accomplish tasks and solve problems in areas where you may not have had direct work experience.

 **Brainstorm with a partner the prior knowledge you have about the following businesses. Consider the types of goods and services provided in each workplace and what employees probably have to do.**

4. Retail store

5. Construction company

6. Doctor's office

7. Bank

8. Post office

## How to Apply What You Know

Once you understand what prior knowledge is and how you can use brainstorming to access that knowledge, you can use it to help you succeed in new workplace situations. Many of these situations will require you to use workplace documents in some way. Use the following steps to help you apply what you know to what you read in workplace documents.

1. **Identify the task.** Establish what you are required to do. Are you completing an assignment? Making a decision? Solving a problem?

2. **Identify what's missing.** Determine what information may be missing from the document. What are you expected to know already?

3. **Apply what you know.** Use what you know to fill in what's missing. Ask yourself how you can use what you know to help you complete the task—and then complete it!

# Develop Your Skills

You often apply prior knowledge to new workplace tasks and problems without even thinking about it. However, the 3-step strategy from the previous page is a useful tool if you need additional help. Let's look at each step individually and then see how they work together.

## Identify the Task

The first step in the 3-step strategy is to determine what you are supposed to do. The task might be written in a document or communicated verbally by a supervisor, co-worker, or customer.

 **The e-mail below was sent to the receptionist at a law firm. Read the e-mail and answer the questions.**

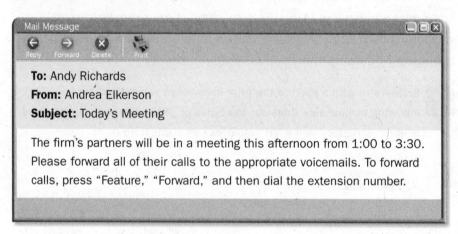

Mail Message

Reply    Forward    Delete    Print

**To:** Andy Richards
**From:** Andrea Elkerson
**Subject:** Today's Meeting

The firm's partners will be in a meeting this afternoon from 1:00 to 3:30. Please forward all of their calls to the appropriate voicemails. To forward calls, press "Feature," "Forward," and then dial the extension number.

**1.** What is Mr. Richards required to do?

## Identify What's Missing

Workplace documents often assume that you already have some knowledge, and they may not provide all of the information that you need to know. If you read a document and are not sure if you have all the information you need to complete the task, think about what information is missing. This will get you one step closer to completing the task.

 **Refer to the e-mail above and answer the following questions.**

**2.** What information does Mr. Richards need in order to complete the task described?

**3.** Which of these pieces of information are in the document, and which are missing?

## Apply What You Know

If information is missing that will prevent you from completing your task, think about what you already know. Do you know some or all of the missing information? Do you know where you can find it? Once you identify helpful prior knowledge, you can apply it to successfully carry out your task.

 **Reread the e-mail on the previous page. Use the statement below to determine if Mr. Richards will be able to complete the task.**

**4.** Mr. Richards knows who each partner in the firm is, and he has a list of all of the law firm's extension numbers.

## Put It All Together

Each step in the 3-step strategy helps you apply knowledge to new contexts. Refer to the scenario and chart below for another example.

Ricco is preparing for his first day as a bank teller. Before starting work, he noticed in the employee handbook that employees must wear "professional clothes." It didn't give any examples, so he isn't sure how to dress.

| Identify the task. | Dress appropriately for work |
| Identify what's missing. | Examples of professional clothes |
| Apply what you know. | Ricco knows most male bank tellers wear slacks and a dress shirt, so that is what he wears. |

 **Read the following document and complete the chart.**

### ANNOUNCEMENT

Please contact the Human Resources department before Monday, August 17, to update your contact information and emergency contacts.

| **5.** Identify the task. | |
| **6.** Identify what's missing. | |
| **7.** Apply what you know. | |

**GOT IT?** **Use these steps to apply prior knowledge to new workplace tasks and solve new problems:**

- Identify what you are supposed to do.
- Identify missing information that prevents you from completing your task.
- Think about and apply what you know to complete the task.

**To-Do List**

Remember to follow these steps when applying your knowledge:

❏ **Identify the task.**

❏ **Identify what's missing.**

❏ **Apply what you know.**

# Apply Your Knowledge

When you are asked to complete a new task using a workplace document, remember to identify exactly what you are supposed to do, determine what information you need to accomplish it, and use your prior knowledge.

**Read each of the following scenarios and its corresponding document. Select the correct response for each question.**

1. Isaiah works in the clothing department at a store. To prepare for back-to-school shopping, the sales manager has asked employees in every department to pull extra stock from the storeroom and shelve it. Isaiah and the other employees receive this list of items and quantities to be shelved.

| Item | Backpacks | Toasters | Pillows | Notebooks | Sweatshirts |
|------|-----------|----------|---------|-----------|-------------|
| Quantity | 6 units | 4 boxes | 8 units | 12 boxes | 5 cases |

**Based on the information in the chart, Isaiah should pull and shelve:**

A. Backpacks

B. Pillows

C. Notebooks

D. Sweatshirts

2. What prior knowledge does Isaiah need in order to complete the task?

3. The smoothie store where you work printed coupons in several newspapers. A customer orders two smoothies and hands you two of these coupons.

**Real Smooth Smoothie Shop**

Buy one smoothie and get a second smoothie free!

Limit one coupon per customer per visit. Offer good at participating shops. No cash value. Promotion Code: XY12

**Based on the information in the scenario and the coupon, you should:**

A. Give the customer cash for the second coupon since she can't use it.

B. Tell the customer that she only needs one coupon for her order.

C. Explain to the customer that there is a limit of one coupon per customer.

D. Double the order since the customer has two coupons.

4. A child at the day care center where you work says he feels sick. You take his temperature and find that it is 101° F. You decide to read the illness policy in the employee handbook to help you decide what to do.

> **Illness Policy**—In order to promote a healthy environment for children and staff, we ask that parents not leave children at the day care center if the child has one or more of the following: fever, extreme vomiting or diarrhea, contagious rash or disease as diagnosed by a doctor, or severe cold or flu symptoms. If a child develops any of the listed symptoms or illnesses while in our care, parents will be called and asked to pick up their child immediately.

**Based on what you know about the child and what you read, you should:**

**A.** Tell the parents that the child should have stayed home.

**B.** Assume that the child will feel better soon.

**C.** Contact the parents and send the child home right away.

**D.** Explain to the child that he is not sick enough to go home.

## In Real Life   Put Your Skills to Work!

You are a landscaper for a city park. Your supervisor has asked you to prepare written instructions for a crew that will be preparing a plot of land for some new trees. He tells you where the plot is located, the members of the crew, and the supplies they will need. Develop the instructions as your supervisor has requested.

 **Think about the problem you are facing and put your skills to work! What is your task? What do you need to know to complete the task? What are you expected to know already?**

### Workplace Tip

When preparing to complete the task, think about:

- Information you need to know
- Information that is given to you and information that may be missing
- What you already know

## Think About It!

**What knowledge do you have that you could apply to new workplace situations?**

Applying your prior knowledge and experiences to new workplace situations can help you accomplish tasks and solve problems at work. Practice identifying what you need to know and filling in some of the missing information with what you know already.

**Answer Key**

**1.** D

**2.** He needs to know that sweatshirts are in the clothing department.

**3.** B

**4.** C

# Test Your WRC Skills

**Apply what you know when you use workplace documents in new situations. Read the following scenarios and review each document. Select the answer you think best responds to the question.**

1. Lakisha works in the information kiosk at the mall. A shopper approaches her and asks where he could buy a basketball. According to the mall floor plan below, Lakisha will probably direct the customer to which store?

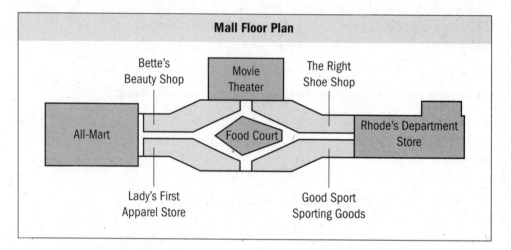

**Mall Floor Plan**

Bette's Beauty Shop

Movie Theater

The Right Shoe Shop

All-Mart

Food Court

Rhode's Department Store

Lady's First Apparel Store

Good Sport Sporting Goods

| A. | ○ | The Right Shoe Shop |
| B. | ○ | Good Sport Sporting Goods |
| C. | ○ | Bette's Beauty Shop |
| D. | ○ | Lady's First Apparel Store |

2. A customer arrives at the dry cleaner where you work to drop off a prom gown. How much should you charge the customer?

| Price List | Shirt | Shorts | Sweater | Skirt | Dress (casual) | Dress (fancy) | Pants | Suit |
|---|---|---|---|---|---|---|---|---|
| | $5.00 | $4.00 | $6.00 | $6.00 | $10.00 | $15.00 | $6.00 | $12.00 |

| A. | ○ | $5.00 |
| B. | ○ | $6.00 |
| C. | ○ | $10.00 |
| D. | ○ | $15.00 |

3. You maintain the medical records at a doctor's office. The father of an 8-year-old patient wants to send his daughter's immunization record to the school nurse. According to this policy, what should you tell the father?

> **Medical Records Transfer Policy:** All individuals or health care providers requesting the medical records of patients must first complete a Medical Records Release Form. Once the patient or patient's guardian (if the patient is a minor) completes this form, the records will be transferred within 5 business days.

A. ○ His daughter must complete the Medical Records Release Form.
B. ○ He should ask the school nurse to fill out the Medical Records Release Form.
C. ○ The Medical Records Release Form can only be completed by the doctor.
D. ○ He must complete the Medical Records Release Form.

4. You work at a convenience store, and it is your responsibility to log the total number of orders received. Your supervisor wants to know how many cases of beverages were delivered. Based on this receiving report, what should you tell her?

| RECEIVING REPORT | | |
| --- | --- | --- |
| Product | Unit of Measure | Quantity |
| Soda | Case | 12 |
| Chocolate bars | Case | 5 |
| Chips | Case | 8 |
| Gum | Case | 6 |

A. ○ 12
B. ○ 5
C. ○ 8
D. ○ 6

5. Milo works as telemarketer for a phone service provider. A consumer has just hung up on Milo upon realizing that the call was a solicitation. Milo glances at the following memo posted by his desk. Based on the memo, what should Milo do?

> **To:** All Employees
> **From:** Jolene Bernstein, Manager
> **RE:** No-Call List
> This is a reminder to all employees that verbal requests, such as "Stop calling" and "Don't call again," and nonverbal actions that demonstrate lack of interest should be recorded. Then the consumer should be placed on our internal "No-Call List." Please contact me if you have questions.

A. ○ Tell Jolene Bernstein, his manager, and then record the incident.
B. ○ Call the consumer back so that he isn't placed on the "No-Call List."
C. ○ Place the consumer's information on the internal "No-Call List."
D. ○ Ignore the memo because the consumer didn't say "Don't call again."

Check your answers on page 172.

# Synthesize Information from Multiple Sources

## Build on What You Know

When you put together a puzzle, you carefully consider how each piece of the puzzle works together to create a complete image. Similarly, when you **synthesize** information from one or more sources, you collect pieces of information and put them together with what you already know to help you form a conclusion or opinion about something.

Synthesizing information is a valuable strategy in the workplace. When you synthesize information, you combine prior knowledge with new information from various sources in order to generate new ideas. Doing so can help you better understand workplace texts, solve problems, and more efficiently manage your job responsibilities.

In this lesson, you will practice synthesizing information in workplace documents to help you better understand their overall meaning.

### Essential Tasks

**Use prior knowledge** and information from reading work-related texts to accomplish reading purpose

**Use prior knowledge** of workplace culture and priorities to interpret text

### In Real Life — What's Your Policy?

Julia recently started as a cashier at an electronics store. A customer has approached her with a DVD player he would like to return. He doesn't have his receipt, and the DVD player is not in its original packaging. However, the customer does have the credit card he used for the purchase. Julia decides to check the store's return policy.

### Bee's Electronics Return Policy

- Returns are allowed only on unused items accompanied by a receipt.
- Returns must be made within 60 days of original purchase date.

 =

**Discuss the following questions. Share your ideas with the class.**

1. Which information in the document will probably help Julia understand what action to take?

2. How do the graphics help clarify the store's return policy?

3. Why do you think it's important for a store to have a return policy?

**Teacher Reminder**
Review the teacher lesson at
www.mysteckvaughn.com/WORK

## Summarize to Synthesize

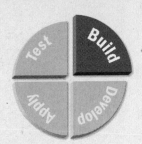

In Lesson 10, you learned that summarizing helps you understand, remember, and share what you read. Summarizing is also an important part of synthesizing information. You can't synthesize without first understanding the main points of what you read.

However, one key difference between summarizing and synthesizing is that summarizing usually takes place at the end of a text, after you have already read it. Synthesizing, on the other hand, occurs throughout the entire reading process. When you synthesize information, you identify and summarize the main idea and details of texts and graphics while also using what you know to draw conclusions about important concepts and the overall meaning.

## Using Multiple Sources

When trying to solve a problem in the workplace, you may not always find the information you need in one location. You may need to review multiple documents in order to know what action is required. When reviewing multiple documents or graphics, you can piece together information from the sources and then use what you already know to make a decision about what action to take next.

 **Review the following e-mail. Then answer the questions and share your ideas with the class.**

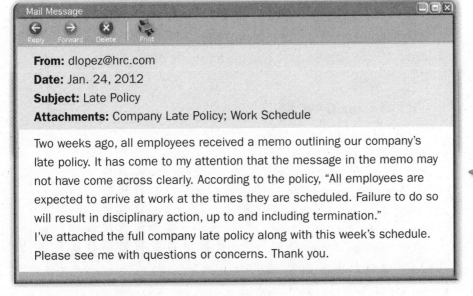

**From:** dlopez@hrc.com
**Date:** Jan. 24, 2012
**Subject:** Late Policy
**Attachments:** Company Late Policy; Work Schedule

Two weeks ago, all employees received a memo outlining our company's late policy. It has come to my attention that the message in the memo may not have come across clearly. According to the policy, "All employees are expected to arrive at work at the times they are scheduled. Failure to do so will result in disciplinary action, up to and including termination."
I've attached the full company late policy along with this week's schedule. Please see me with questions or concerns. Thank you.

> **Workplace Tip**
> Drawing conclusions from what you read can help you with understanding your workplace culture and priorities. You can also use what you already know to understand what you read in the workplace.

4. What documents are referenced in the e-mail?

5. Based on what you read and what you know, what actions would you take to obey the policy?

6. How does this e-mail help you understand this work environment and its priorities?

# Develop Your Skills

Remember, to synthesize information from one or more sources, you must put together the new information with your prior knowledge to draw a conclusion about the overall meaning.

## Put the Puzzle Together

You already know how to summarize the main idea and details of a text. You've also learned to make inferences about information that may not be directly stated. When you synthesize, or put all the pieces together, you will have a complete picture to guide your actions and help you succeed in the workplace.

The following Summarize-to-Synthesize chart may help you piece together information and draw the most meaning from workplace documents.

| Summarize → | Use Prior Knowledge → | Synthesize |
|---|---|---|
| Summarize the information from each source. | Use what you know to make observations or ask questions. | Put the pieces together to understand the overall meaning. |

Once you have organized important points and your own thoughts and questions, you can combine what you've learned with what you already know to form a conclusion or to determine what action you should take.

 **Read the following document. Use the Summarize-to-Synthesize chart to help you answer the questions.**

Anthony is training to work as a central air conditioning and heating repairman. His supervisor gave him the following document.

### Notice About Overtime

Business may be slow some months and very busy other months. Please note that during the peak months, employees may be required to work overtime to manage the additional workload. Employees will be compensated for all overtime hours.

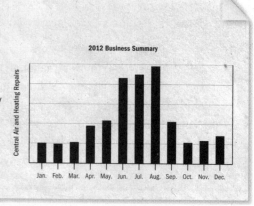

2012 Business Summary

1. How would you summarize each source to share the information with a co-worker?

2. What information from the bar graph can you use to better understand the text next to it?

3. During which months will Anthony have to work the most overtime?

# Additional Tips for Synthesizing Information

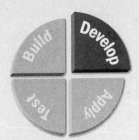

Along with using a Summarize-to-Synthesize chart, keep the following tips in mind. They will help you understand new information, apply prior knowledge, and draw conclusions.

- Read sources carefully, stopping sometimes to organize your thoughts.

- Identify the main idea and details of each source.

- Summarize and respond to each source in your own words.

- Use prior knowledge and what you have learned to help you understand the overall meaning.

 **Read the memo and discuss the questions with a classmate.**

## Memo

**To:** Landscapers
**From:** Murray's Management
**Re:** Seasonal Inventory

This memo is to remind you that some plants fare better than others during the hot, dry summer months. We've placed an order for new plants based on their durability and popularity among clients.

Please review the new inventory. Wait until all summer plants have sold before placing orders to update the inventory.

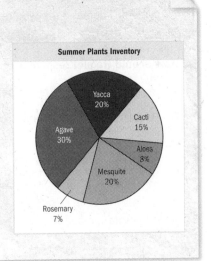

Summer Plants Inventory

Yacca 20%
Cacti 15%
Aloes 8%
Agave 30%
Mesquite 20%
Rosemary 7%

4. What type of summer plant will Murray's probably sell the most of? Why do you think so?

5. What should an employee of Murray's do if a customer requests a type of plant that has sold out?

---

**GOT IT?**

**Synthesizing information can help you understand workplace documents, solve problems, and manage your responsibilities in the workplace. Remember to:**

- Read sources carefully.

- Keep track of each source's main ideas.

- Use prior knowledge to respond to each source.

- Draw conclusions based on all of the information.

---

**Answer Key**

1. According to the text, employees must work overtime during peak months. The graph shows how busy the company was each month in 2012.

2. According to the graph, employees are busiest during the summer.

3. Anthony will have to work more overtime during June, July, and August.

4. Agave. Together, the text and the graph tell you that agave is the most popular plant among clients.

5. Recommend another type of plant from the inventory, or if all other plants are sold out, order more.

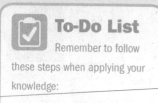
# Apply Your Knowledge

Use the strategies you've learned to synthesize information.

**Read each of the following scenarios and workplace documents. Select the correct response for each question.**

1. Raquel works for a hardware company. Her main responsibility is to make sure all customers are fully satisfied. She receives the following e-mail.

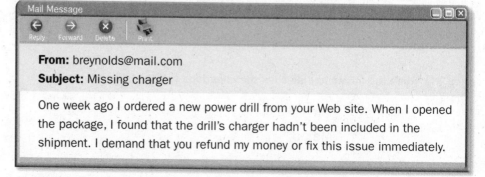

Mail Message

Reply   Forward   Delete   Print

**From:** breynolds@mail.com
**Subject:** Missing charger

One week ago I ordered a new power drill from your Web site. When I opened the package, I found that the drill's charger hadn't been included in the shipment. I demand that you refund my money or fix this issue immediately.

**How should Raquel respond to the customer's complaint?**

A. Report the e-mail to her supervisor because the customer was rude.

B. Request that the customer return the drill for a full refund.

C. Apologize and send the missing charger as soon as possible.

D. Contact her supervisors so they can meet to discuss the problem.

2. What information about Raquel's job helped you answer question 1?

3. Burke wants to get a Commercial Driver's License so he can help transport deliveries. His supervisor gives him the following document.

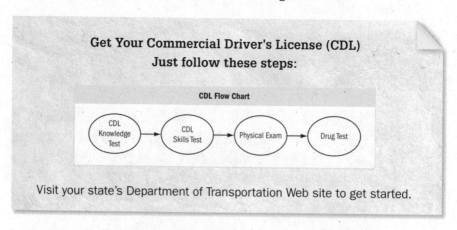

**Get Your Commercial Driver's License (CDL)**
**Just follow these steps:**

CDL Flow Chart

CDL Knowledge Test → CDL Skills Test → Physical Exam → Drug Test

Visit your state's Department of Transportation Web site to get started.

**What should Burke do first after signing up to qualify for his CDL?**

A. Begin studying to prepare for the CDL Knowledge Test

B. Ask his supervisor to teach him how to drive a delivery truck

C. Begin training to pass the physical exam

D. Ask his supervisor to write him a letter of recommendation

**4.** Sun prepares sushi at a popular restaurant. She receives this memo.

> **To:** All Food Preparers
> **From:** Management
> **Re:** Large Catering Order
>
> This memo is to inform you of a large order that has been placed. The following dishes must be prepared for a catered dinner that will take place tomorrow.

| Dish | Quantity |
| --- | --- |
| Dinner Salad | 50 |
| Chicken Special | 27 |
| Beef Special | 23 |
| Sushi Roll | 25 |
| Soup | 25 |

**What is Sun responsible for preparing?**

**A.** 50 dinner salads

**B.** 27 chicken specials

**C.** 23 beef specials

**D.** 25 sushi rolls

## In Real Life Put Your Skills to Work!

You are a customer service agent at an amusement park. Part of your job is to know which attractions guests of different ages will enjoy, as well as where all refreshment stands and restrooms are located. Your boss has asked you to create a map to help new agents direct guests around the park. Create a map as your boss has requested.

 **Think about the problem you are facing and put your skills to work! What kinds of information will be on your map? Explain your answers.**

## Think About It!

**What sources of information are the most useful to you on the job?**

You have learned valuable strategies throughout this book to help you understand workplace documents. When you synthesize information, you use many of these strategies at the same time. Synthesizing can help you understand the "big picture" and succeed in your career.

**Answer Key**

**1.** C

**2.** The scenario says that Raquel's job is to make sure customers are fully satisfied.

**3.** A

**4.** D

# Test Your WRC Skills

**Understanding workplace documents requires a variety of reading skills. Read the following scenarios and review each document. Select the answer you think best responds to the question.**

1. You work in the produce department of a grocery store. According to the memo, which items from the list should you mark with sale prices?

---

**MEMO**

**To:** Department Managers

**From:** Management

**RE:** Stocking Items for the Thanksgiving Holiday

With Thanksgiving fast approaching, certain items have been marked down from their normal prices. Please mark the items in your department with their sale prices.

| Item | Sale Price |
|---|---|
| Turkey | $1.39 /lb |
| 9" pie shells (2 pack) | $1.49 |
| Sweet Potatoes | $0.70 /lb |
| Whole milk (gallon) | $2.36 |

---

A. ◯ Turkey

B. ◯ Pie shells

C. ◯ Sweet potatoes

D. ◯ Whole milk

2. You work as a welder. Recently, you have seen this notice posted in several work areas. What is the **MAIN** idea of this sign?

---

**SAFETY NOTICE**

Though workplace injuries are uncommon, we are ALL responsible for keeping the work environment safe. Please maintain a clean workspace at all times and follow company procedures and dress codes. If you notice a hazard or safety risk, please notify your supervisor immediately.

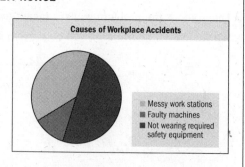

Causes of Workplace Accidents

■ Messy work stations
■ Faulty machines
■ Not wearing required safety equipment

---

A. ◯ Take responsibility for the safety of your work environment.

B. ◯ Follow the rules, even if there is no good reason to do so.

C. ◯ Keep the workplace clean for a more attractive work environment.

D. ◯ There have been too many workplace accidents recently.

3. You just began working as a painter. Your supervisor explains that you need to be careful to avoid the paint problems shown in the sign below. According to the sign, what should you do if you have to paint over an oil-based finish with a water-based paint?

For painters who must cover an oil-based finish with a water-based paint, the wall will first need to be primed with an oil-based primer. Failure to do so will result in problems with the paint finish.

**Possible Paint Problems**

| | | |
|---|---|---|
| **A.** ⚪ | Peel the oil-based paint from the wall. | |
| **B.** ⚪ | Prime the wall with an oil-based primer. | |
| **C.** ⚪ | Prime any parts of the wall that are peeling. | |
| **D.** ⚪ | Prime the wall with water-based paint. | |

4. A customer has a nail in her car tire, and the tire needs to be repaired or replaced. The model number is 940614. If you cannot repair the tire, what should you do?

| Model Number | In Stock | Most comparable* | Warranty Note |
|---|---|---|---|
| 940614 | 0 | 947623 | *If a tire model is not in stock, |
| 920316 | 12 | 958473 | please recommend the most |
| 947623 | 7 | 940614 | comparable model to customers |
| 939485 | 14 | 958382 | and provide a 10% discount. |

| | | |
|---|---|---|
| **A.** ⚪ | Place an order for model number 940614. | |
| **B.** ⚪ | Repair the tire and offer the customer a 10% discount. | |
| **C.** ⚪ | Recommend models 920316 or 939485. | |
| **D.** ⚪ | Recommend model 947623 and offer a 10% discount. | |

5. You work at a jewelry store. A customer who purchased a ring from your store last year has requested a free ring cleaning. According to this policy, what should you do?

**Free Jewelry Cleaning**

Customers purchasing new jewelry may have one other piece of jewelry cleaned free of charge. Offer valid only with new purchase.

| | | |
|---|---|---|
| **A.** ⚪ | Give her a free ring cleaning. | |
| **B.** ⚪ | Explain that the offer is valid only with a new purchase. | |
| **C.** ⚪ | Inspect her ring to see if it needs cleaning. | |
| **D.** ⚪ | Ask for a copy of her receipt before cleaning her ring. | |

Check your answers on page 173.

# Skills for the Workplace

## Workplace Jargon

Have you ever watched a medical TV show? If so, you have probably heard lines such as, "Get me a CBC, Chem 7, and tox screen, stat!" You don't need to understand what those medical words mean to enjoy the show. But if you worked in a hospital emergency room, you would need to learn them.

Every workplace uses **jargon**, or words that are unfamiliar to people who work outside that industry or job. Workplace jargon that is used across many types of businesses is called business jargon or corporate jargon. Some examples of jargon include:

**Hospital or Doctor's Office**

- Chart: a patient's medical records
- Stat: right away, immediately
- Vitals: vital signs, such as pulse and temperature

**Restaurant**

- Four-top: a table for four
- Campers: people who stay too long
- Sidework: work that servers do when not serving guests

## Workplace Scenario

What does the following common workplace jargon mean?

- FYI  *For your information*
- ASAP  *As soon as possible*
- ETA  *Estimated time of arrival*
- Action items  *Things that need to be done*
- Touch base  *To check in and communicate on a subject*

When you start a new job, you may hear or read words, abbreviations, and phrases you have never heard before. Learning this new vocabulary will help you succeed at your job. What are some ways to learn this new vocabulary?

**Do Your Research** Read all you can about the company where you work. Search online for "medical jargon," "legal jargon," or other types of jargon.

**Use Clues** Look for clues such as definitions, synonyms, antonyms, and examples that can help you figure out the meaning of an unfamiliar term.

**Keep a List** Write down terms you hear or read that you don't understand. Look them up later or ask a supervisor or co-worker to define them for you.

# Workplace Practice

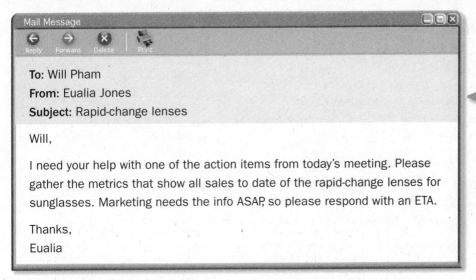

## Workplace Tip

Keep in mind that e-mails in the workplace are often written quickly, so they are more informal than longer documents. To save time, someone may use abbreviations and jargon when writing e-mails.

- Should Will respond to this e-mail before finding the information? *Yes. He needs to give an estimate for how long it will take him to gather the information Eualia has requested.*

- What are metrics, and how do you know? *Metrics are data that measure something—in this case, how many rapid-change lenses have been sold. The phrase "that show all sales to date" provides a clue to the term's meaning.*

## It's Your Turn!

1. You just got a job at a parcel delivery company. What can you do ahead of time to help you on your first day of work?

2. At your new job at a dental office, one of your responsibilities is to order supplies. The dentist tells you that bitewing tabs are running low. What are two ways you can find out what to order?

3. The employee handbook for your new job at a hotel describes several situations in which employees should contact the MOD. You can't figure out what a "MOD" is. What should you do?

4. You are training for a job and read that you must complete at least 50 simulated transactions before taking the cashier's test. How many customers will you check out before the test?

**It's Your Turn! Answer Key**
1. Go online and read common jargon used in delivery companies.
2. Go to the supply closet and look for the bitewing tabs. Ask the dentist or a co-worker.
3. Since you need to know this term to do your job, you should look it up or ask your manager what it means.
4. None. The word *simulated* means that the transactions are not real.

# Chapter 5 Assessment

**Select the answer you think best responds to the question.**

**1.** A customer asks you the discount on a brush for her cat. What should you tell her?

> ### MEMO
>
> **To:** All Department Managers
> **From:** Andrea Esposito, Pet Town Store Manager
> **RE:** Everything-Must-Go Sale
>
> We are pleased to announce our annual Everything-Must-Go sale! To prepare for customers' questions about our sales, please distribute this chart at your team meeting.
>
> | | | |
> |---|---|---|
> | **Fish Department** | Tanks/Bowls | 40% off |
> | | Food: Flakes and Pellets | 15% off |
> | **Dog Department** | Grooming Supplies | 30% off |
> | | Toys | 20% off |
> | | Food: Wet and Dry | 15% off |
> | **Cat Department** | Grooming Supplies | 20% off |
> | | Toys | 60% off |
> | | Food: Wet and Dry | 20% off |

A. ○ The item is 10% off.

B. ○ The item is 20% off.

C. ○ The item is 30% off.

D. ○ The item is not on sale.

**2.** You are an assistant manager at Value Dollar. A customer wants to buy one item and asks you if he can use two coupons from Grocery Mart. What should you tell the customer?

> **Value Dollar's Price-Match Guarantee**
>
> We gladly accept all competitors' coupons! *
>
> *We do not accept expired coupons.
>
> *Limit one coupon per item, per purchase.

A. ○ Tell the customer that he cannot use Grocery Mart coupons.

B. ○ Accept both of the customer's coupons.

C. ○ Tell the customer that you cannot accept expired coupons.

D. ○ Explain that the customer may use one coupon.

**3.** You accidentally charge a customer twice for an item. Before you can fix the problem, your cash register shuts down. You remember seeing the notice below. What should you do?

---

### NOTICE

This morning our electronic cash registers have been experiencing technical problems. Our tech department is working on the problem. Please do what you can to keep this problem from inconveniencing our customers.

---

| | | |
|---|---|---|
| **A.** | ○ | Call a manager for assistance and try to restart the cash register. |
| **B.** | ○ | Let the customer take all of her purchases without paying for them. |
| **C.** | ○ | Void the transaction and rescan the purchases. |
| **D.** | ○ | Ask the customer to come back later. |

**4.** You work for a shoe company that strives to provide excellent customer service. You receive this e-mail from a customer. What would be the **MOST** appropriate response?

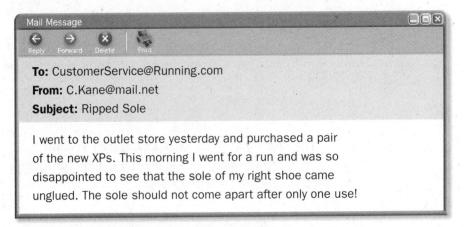

Mail Message

Reply   Forward   Delete   Print

**To:** CustomerService@Running.com
**From:** C.Kane@mail.net
**Subject:** Ripped Sole

I went to the outlet store yesterday and purchased a pair of the new XPs. This morning I went for a run and was so disappointed to see that the sole of my right shoe came unglued. The sole should not come apart after only one use!

| | | |
|---|---|---|
| **A.** | ○ | Forward the e-mail and picture to a co-worker. |
| **B.** | ○ | Respond that purchases at outlet stores cannot be refunded. |
| **C.** | ○ | Send an apology e-mail with a coupon for a new pair of shoes. |
| **D.** | ○ | Tell the customer to take the shoes back to the outlet store. |

**5.** If you are a non-disabled employee, where would be the **BEST** place for you to park tomorrow?

---

**Attention Employees:** Parking Garage B will be undergoing repairs tomorrow. As a result, most handicapped parking spaces will be unavailable to our disabled employees. We have reserved Level 1 of Garage A for them. Now non-disabled employees should use Levels 2–5 of Garage A.

---

| | | |
|---|---|---|
| **A.** | ○ | Parking Garage B, Level 1 |
| **B.** | ○ | Parking Garage B, Level 2 |
| **C.** | ○ | Parking Garage A, Level 1 |
| **D.** | ○ | Parking Garage A, Level 2 |

Check your answers on page 173.

 For more Chapter 5 assessment questions, please visit www.mysteckvaughn.com/WORK

# WorkSkills™ Glossary

The following words were used in the WorkSkills™ Reading book. Knowing these words will help you as you study for the National Work Readiness Credential assessment.

## — A

**Antonym** (**an**-tuh-nim) a word that means the opposite of another word

**Audience** (**aw**-dee-uhns) the intended readers of a piece of writing

**Author** (**aw**-ther) the writer of a text

## — C

**Cause** (kawz) something that brings about a change or result

**Columns** (**kol**-uhmz) items arranged in vertical lines

**Compare** (kuhm-**pair**) to explain how two or more things are alike

**Context** (**kon**-tekst) the overall meaning of a document

**Context clues** (**kon**-tekst klooz) hints in a text that can help readers define unknown or unfamiliar words

**Contrast** (**kon**-trast) to explain how two or more things are different

**Critical reading** (**krit**-i-kuhl **ree**-ding) thinking about the underlying meaning of a text either during or after reading

## — D

**Database** (**dey**-tuh-beys) a collection of data, or information, that is usually stored on a computer; set up so that information can be easily sorted and located

**Directional signs** (**dih**-rek-shuh-nl sahynz) signs that show you where something is or how to get somewhere

**Documents** (**dok**-yuh-muhnts) written texts that provide information about something

## — E

**Effect** (**ih**-fekt) something that happens as a result of something else

**Effective** (ih-**fek**-tiv) successful at achieving the intended purpose

## — F

**Facts** (fakts) statements that can be proven to be true

## — G

**Graphic displays** (**graf**-ik dih-**spleyz**) visual representations of information that use format, words, and images

## — H

**Health and safety signs** (helth and **seyf**-tee sahynz) signs that keep you safe by warning you of danger, telling you what to do in an emergency, or protecting you from illness or injury

## — I

**Inferences** (**in**-fer-uhns-ez) thoughts and ideas concluded or guessed at based on available information and prior knowledge

**Informational signs** (in-fer-**mey**-shuhn-al sahynz) signs that give you basic information, such as who, what, when, where, or why

**Instructional signs** (in-**struhk**-shuhn-al sahynz) signs that explain how to do something

## J

**Jargon** (**jahr**-guhn) the special words and phrases used in a particular line of work

## M

**Main idea** (meyn ahy-**dee**-uh) the most important point or key concept of something, such as a document

**Minutes** (**min**-its) a short written record of what happened in a meeting

## O

**Opinions** (uh-**pin**-yuhnz) statements of a person's thoughts, feelings, or beliefs, which cannot be proven

## P

**Predict** (pri-**dikt**) to tell about something in advance of when it happens

**Prefix** (**pree**-fiks) a letter or group of letters that comes at the beginning of a word and changes the word's meaning

**Preview** (**pree**-vyoo) to look at a text's structure and content before reading it in depth

**Prior knowledge** (**prahy**-er **nol**-ij) what you already know about something

**Purpose** (**pur**-puhs) the aim, goal, or use of something

## R

**Root** (root) a word or part of a word from which other words are formed

**Rows** (rohz) items arranged in horizontal lines

## S

**Scan** (skan) to find specific information in a text

**Sequence** (**see**-kwuhns) the order in which things are arranged or connected

**Signal words** (**sig**-nl wurdz) key words that can guide readers to important information in texts

**Skim** (skim) to quickly find the main idea without reading every word

**Strategies** (**strat**-i-jeez) methods or plans of action used to accomplish specific goals

**Suffix** (**suhf**-iks) a letter or group of letters that comes at the end of a word and changes the word's meaning

**Summary** (**suhm**-uh-ree) a short review of the main points and key details

**Supporting details** (suh-**pawrt**-ing dih-**teylz**) pieces of information that support the main idea or key concept

**Synonym** (**sin**-uh-nim) a word that has the same or almost the same meaning as another word

**Synopsis** (si-**nop**-sis) a brief outline or summary

**Synthesize** (**sin**-thuh-sahyz) to form an idea by combining prior knowledge and information from one or more sources

## T

**Text features** (tekst **fee**-cherz) text with special styling or placement, such as headings, bold print, italics, and lists

**Troubleshooting** (**truhb**-uhl-shoot-ing) the process of identifying a problem and trying to find a solution

## V

**Visuals** (**vizh**-oo-uhlz) images, such as graphics or pictures, used to show or explain something

# Answers and Explanations

Lesson 1 Test Your WRC Skills (pages 20–21)

**1. C. Prepare for stormy weather by dressing warmly.**
Option C is correct. The final line of the memo explains what all mail carriers should do. Option A is incorrect because supervisors will assign new routes. Option B is incorrect because mail carriers are not being asked to work faster. Option D is incorrect because the memo states that supervisors already are aware of the situation and are going to distribute shortened routes.

**2. D. You receive holiday pay plus your regular pay.**
Option D is correct. The first line of the policy explains that employees who agree to work on a paid holiday receive both regular and holiday pay. Options A and C are incorrect because they confuse other parts of the text with the specific policy in question. Option B is incorrect because employees receive both holiday and regular pay.

**3. B. 5**
Option B is correct. Manuel is scheduled to work 5 days. Options A, C, and D are incorrect because they do not reflect the information on the schedule.

**4. D. Filing inventory and prescription records**
Option D is correct. Inventory and prescription records must be filed. Option A is incorrect because prescription labels must be prepared and typed, not unpacked. Option B is incorrect because deliveries must be received, not prepared. Option C is incorrect because incoming items must be unpacked and labeled, not sorted.

**5. A. Khaki pants**
Option A is correct. The *Quantity* column shows that 4 pairs of khaki pants were ordered, which is more than any other item. Option B is incorrect because only 2 blue blazers were ordered. Option C is incorrect because only 1 pair of black shoes was ordered. Option D is incorrect because only 3 striped ties were ordered.

Lesson 2 Test Your WRC Skills (pages 28–29)

**1. B. E-mail and Internet use are for work-related tasks only.**
Option B is correct. Both paragraphs of the policy indicate that computer use is for work-related tasks only. Option A is incorrect because employees may access e-mail and Internet on work computers for work purposes. Option C is not correct because employees can use e-mail for work purposes. Option D is incorrect because e-mail and Internet access are available on work computers.

**2. C. 8**
Option C is correct. The customer ordered 8 gallons of green paint. Options A, B, and D are incorrect because they show how many gallons of yellow paint, brown stain, and white primer the customer ordered.

**3. A. To announce an inspection that will affect crane operators' schedules**
Option A is correct because the memo announces an inspection that affects crane operators' work schedules. Option B is incorrect because crane operators are expected to return to work at 1:00 on Thursday. Option C is incorrect because crane operators will not be inspecting their cranes. Option D is incorrect because the memo does not mention crane repairs.

**4. B. Women are entitled to return to their original job after pregnancy.**
Option B is correct. The first sentence of the policy explains that women may return to their original position. Option A, while true, is not the correct answer because it is not the main idea of the document. Option C is incorrect because it is not necessary for women to reapply for their jobs. Option D, while true, is not correct because it is not the main idea of the document.

**5. D. Check in the equipment.**
Option D is correct. The flyer reminds you to check in equipment and cross your name off the sign-out sheet. Option A is incorrect because you should return the equipment yourself, not ask a supervisor. Option B is incorrect because you sign out the equipment when you check it out, not when you are done with it. Option C is incorrect because you should not loan out equipment that is checked out under your name.

## Chapter 1 Assessment (pages 32–33)

### 1. C. To encourage employees to help reduce energy costs in the building

Option C is correct. The main purpose of the document is to encourage employees to help the company save energy. Options A and B are incorrect because printing documents on scrap paper and shutting down computers are specific ways employees can save energy. They are not the main purpose of the document. Option D is incorrect because the document asks employees to turn off lights in vacant conference rooms, not to put the rooms to better use.

### 2. B. Remove the pan from the stove and drain the water.

Option B is correct. Steps 7 and 8 indicate that employees should remove the pan from the stove and then drain the water when the timer goes off. Option A is incorrect because employees washing their hands with soap is the first step of the lab procedure. Option C is incorrect because these steps are in the incorrect order and also occur before the timer goes off. Option D is incorrect because employees must remove the pan from the stove and drain the water before letting the equipment cool.

### 3. D. R. Emery

Option D is correct. The fourth column of the log says that R. Emery returned laptop 2156-A on 2/19/2012. Option A is incorrect because J. Hernandez returned laptop 2156-A on 2/14/2012, not 2/19/2012. Option B is incorrect because O. Miller borrowed a different computer and returned it on a different date. Option C is incorrect because A. Gilbert borrowed laptop 2156-C, not 2156-A.

### 4. A. To outline the policy for employees who would like to transfer

Option A is correct. The purpose of the memo is to outline the policy for employees who wish to transfer to a different location. Option B is incorrect because the memo does not mention the size of the stores. Option C is incorrect because the memo does not explain the new schedule at the downtown store. Option D is incorrect because the memo does not encourage employees to work at a specific location.

### 5. C. Yellow badge

Option C is correct. The sign states that employees with a yellow badge may be admitted to Work Sites A and C. No other badge grants admittance to Work Site C. Option A is incorrect because the admittance rules say that employees with a green badge may be admitted to Work Site A only. Option B is incorrect because employees with a blue badge may be admitted to Work Sites B and D, but not C. Option D is incorrect because employees with an orange badge may be admitted to Work Site B only.

## Lesson 3 Test Your WRC Skills (pages 42–43)

### 1. C. Information about the music download policy

Option C is correct. The subject of the e-mail is "Music Download Policy," which tells you that the e-mail will include information about this particular policy. Option A is not correct because the subject does not imply that you will learn how to download music. Option B is incorrect because it refers to the e-mail's sender, not the subject. Option D is incorrect because the subject mentions only one policy.

### 2. D. Click SAVE.

Option D is correct. The instructions for naming a document are listed in the order that they should occur. The last step is number 6, "Click SAVE." Options A, B, and C are incorrect because they are all steps that occur before clicking SAVE.

### 3. A. All temporary and permanent employees

Option A is correct. The bold word "Who" calls out the people who are invited—all temporary and permanent employees. Option B is incorrect because the Human Resources department is hosting the lunch. Option C is not correct because Clarence McDougal is the name of the dining room. Option D is incorrect because Smith and Company is the name of the company.

### 4. C. An important note about receiving alternate routes

Option C is correct. The inclusion of the word "Notice" means that the document will be an important note about something. In this case, the note is about receiving alternate routes. Option A is not correct because a notice is not a reminder. Option B is incorrect because a procedure lists steps, not a notice. Option D is incorrect because a notice is not a policy, which is a document that outlines rules.

### 5. B. Making Your Pitch

Option B is correct. The day of each training session is listed under the title of the session. May 22 is listed under "Making Your Pitch." Options A, C, and D are incorrect because they list the training sessions offered on May 21, May 23, and May 24.

## Lesson 4 Test Your WRC Skills (pages 50–51)

### 1. D. 3066

Option D is correct. The code number in the column next to the item "Pear" is 3066. Option A is incorrect because 3078 is the code number for peaches. Option B is not correct because 3014 is the code number for apples. Option C is incorrect because 3098 is the code number for tangerines.

### 2. D. Home décor

Option D is correct. Home décor takes up over half of the pie chart. This means it makes up over half of the store's inventory. Options A, B, and C are incorrect because they are smaller sections of the pie chart and represent less inventory.

### 3. A. Parts of a forklift

Option A is correct. The diagram of the forklift is labeled to identify its parts. Option B is incorrect because the diagram does not show how to operate the parts of the forklift. Option C is not correct because the diagram shows only one forklift. Option D is not correct because the diagram does not tell you when to use a forklift.

### 4. C. 12:00

Option C is correct. The graph shows that the average number of calls at 12:00 is 25, which is more than any other time of day. Options A, B, and D are incorrect because the average number of calls is less than 25 at those times of the day.

### 5. C. Instructions for using a spirit level

Option C is correct. The words "How to Use" in the title tell you that you will receive instructions for how to do something. Options A and B are incorrect because the title does not indicate that instructions for ordering or making spirit levels will be included. Option D is not correct because cleaning is only one part of the process of using a spirit level.

## Lesson 5 Test Your WRC Skills (pages 58–59)

### 1. D. Mop the floor.

Option D is correct. The second step of the night crew cleaning instructions is to mop the floor. Option A is incorrect because emptying the mop water is the third step of the cleaning instructions. Option B is incorrect because sweeping the floor is the first step of the cleaning instructions. Option C is incorrect because putting away the broom is in the last step of the instructions.

### 2. B. Being on time

Option B is correct. The word *punctual* means being on time. The first two sentences both talk about being on time, giving clues to the meaning of *punctual*. Options A, C, and D are incorrect because *punctual* does not mean cleaning your desk, receiving a letter, or reading a personnel file.

### 3. B. Scanning the patient's insurance card

Option B is correct. Scanning a patient's insurance card is the step before asking if the patient is a new or existing patient. Option A is incorrect because having the patient sign in is two steps before asking if the patient is a new or existing patient. Options C and D are incorrect because handing forms to the patient comes after asking if he or she is a new or existing patient.

### 4. A. Work together

Option A is correct. *Collaborate* means to work together. The term *team up* gives a clue to the meaning of *collaborate*. Options B, C, and D are incorrect because *collaborate* does not mean to write an order form, talk to clients, or run out of time.

### 5. C. Returning the signed request form to the Payroll department

Option C is correct. After your supervisor signs your overtime request form, you must return the signed form to the Payroll department. Options A and B are incorrect because getting the form from the Payroll department and filling out the first three sections of the form are steps that come before your supervisor signs the form. Option D is incorrect because asking your supervisor for permission to work overtime is not a step listed in the reminder.

## Lesson 6 Test Your WRC Skills (pages 66–67)

### 1. C. Give the sandwich to a cashier.
Option C is correct. After they prepare a sandwich, employees must give the sandwich to a cashier. Options A and B are incorrect because employees must complete these steps before they prepare a sandwich. Option D is incorrect because after employees prepare a sandwich, they must give it to a cashier, not the customer.

### 2. B. Thank the customer for shopping at the store.
Option B is correct. The last step of the return procedure is thanking the customer for shopping at the store. Options A, C, and D are incorrect because they all come before thanking the customer for shopping at the store.

### 3. B. S.B.
Option B is correct. S.B. cleaned the fitting room at ten o'clock on Monday. Option A is incorrect because T.L. cleaned the fitting room at 9:00 on Monday, not 10:00. Option C is not correct because K.P. cleaned the fitting room at 10:00 on Tuesday, not Monday. Option D is incorrect because J.T. cleaned the fitting room at 12:00 on Monday, not 10:00.

### 4. D. March 11th
Option D is correct. Group B has computer training on March 11th. Option A is incorrect because Group A has safety training on March 3rd. Option B is incorrect because Group B has safety training on March 4th. Option C is incorrect because Group A has computer training on March 10th.

### 5. A. Fort Worth, TX
Option A is correct. Machine Services, Inc., has jobs in Norman, OK, and Fort Worth, TX. Options B, C, and D are incorrect because Machine Services, Inc., does not have jobs located in Brooklyn, NY, Boston, MA, or Dallas, TX.

## Chapter 2 Assessment (pages 70–71)

### 1. C. Turn in
Option C is correct. *Submit* means "to turn in." The memo is about turning in your time sheet by a certain date. Option A is incorrect because an employee does not need to type the time sheet. Option B is incorrect because if you throw away your time sheet, it will not be processed. Option D is incorrect because although you might print out a time sheet, you would still need to turn it in.

### 2. A. New measures regarding building security
Option A is correct. The notice discusses new building security measures. The measures listed are all related to keeping a building secure. Options B, C, and D are incorrect because these items are neither related to building security nor are they discussed in the notice.

### 3. B. 22.75
Option B is correct. The question asks how many hours Jan worked in total. The row titled "Total Hours" shows 22.75, or the sum of the hours she worked Monday, Tuesday, and Wednesday. Option A is incorrect because 16 is the number of hours Jan worked Monday and Tuesday. Option C is incorrect because 6.75 is the number of hours Jan worked on Wednesday. Option D is incorrect because 8 is the number of hours Jan worked on either Monday or Tuesday.

### 4. D. Place a cloth or plastic tarp on the floor.
Option D is correct. The fourth step is to use large tape to cover edges, and then use blue tape to seal the seam. The step that comes after that is to place a cloth or plastic tarp on the floor. Options A, B, and C are incorrect because those steps come before sealing the edges.

### 5. C. To reduce trash by 50% and help the environment
Option C is correct. The notice asks employees to participate in the recycling program to meet the company's goal of reducing trash by 50%. By doing so, employees will also help save the planet. Option A is incorrect because the notice does not say that the program is mandatory. Options B and D are incorrect because the notice does not discuss janitorial employees or cash rewards for recycling.

## Lesson 7 Test Your WRC Skills (pages 80–81)

**1. A. 8:00 A.M.–10:00 A.M.**
Option A is correct. Aides work with patient records between these times. Option B is incorrect because aides accompany patients outside the facility during these hours. Option C is incorrect because aides change and launder linens during these hours. Option D is incorrect because aides visit with patients during these hours.

**2. C. Slip-resistant footwear**
Option C is correct. The flyer instructs staff to wear slip-resistant footwear. Options A, B, and D are incorrect because the flyer does not mention comfortable footwear, black pants and shirt, or a water-resistant uniform as dress requirements.

**3. D. Employees must wear protective equipment during renovations of Flowers Hall.**
Option D is correct. The memo states that employees working in or near Flowers Hall must wear protective clothing and equipment. Option A is incorrect because the memo does not state when renovations begin. Option B is incorrect because the memo does not call for volunteers to help with the renovations. Option C is incorrect because the memo explains that Flowers Hall is the site of renovations, not a meeting room.

**4. B. Claim ticket**
Option B is correct. The first item of the policy states that employees must give a customer a claim ticket when accepting garments. Options A and C are incorrect because a customer must present a photo ID and signature if the claim ticket is lost. Option D is incorrect because employees are accepting garments, not giving them back to the customer.

**5. D. Wear protective gloves when working in exam rooms.**
Option D is correct. The text on the sign instructs dental assistants to wear protective gloves when examining patients or working in exam rooms. Option A is incorrect because the sign does not address dental assistants studying to become dentists. Option B is incorrect because protective gloves are not required at all times. Option C is incorrect because the sign does not address the procedure for handling instruments in exam rooms.

## Lesson 8 Test Your WRC Skills (pages 88–89)

**1. D. To be excused**
Option D is correct. The word *exempt* in this context means to be excused from something. The phrase "but you must attend . . . tomorrow" gives a clue to the meaning of *exempt*. Options A, B, and C are incorrect because *exempt* does not mean to earn a salary, to attend a meeting, or to sign a time sheet.

**2. B. Changes**
Option B is correct. *Modifications* are changes. The words "these changes" give a clue to the meaning of *modifications*. Options A, C, and D are incorrect because modifications are not holidays, questions, or store hours.

**3. A. Private**
Option A is correct. *Confidential* means private or secret. The phrase "should not be shared with anyone outside of our company" gives a clue to the word's meaning. Options B, C, and D are incorrect because *confidential* does not mean illegal, angry, or offensive.

**4. C. To get to know**
Option C is correct. *Acquaint* means to get to know someone or something. The meaning is stated in the next sentence: "It is very important that you *get to know* all of our safety policies and procedures." Options A, B, and D are incorrect because *acquaint* does not mean to be welcomed, to be safe, or to be part of a team.

**5. B. Not legal**
Option B is correct. *Unlawful* means not legal. The word parts in *unlawful* provide clues to its meaning, as well as the word *prohibited* and the last sentence on the sign. Options A, C, and D are incorrect because *unlawful* does not mean not safe, not finished, or not working.

## Lesson 9 Test Your WRC Skills (pages 96–97)

### 1. B. Healthy employees help the company reduce costs.
Option B is correct. The dollar sign in the center of the diagram, as well as the words at the top of the sign, indicate that staying healthy will save the company money. Options A and C are not correct because the sign does not suggest that individual employees will be reprimanded or punished in any way. Option D is incorrect because these are details in the sign, not the main idea.

### 2. C. To prevent employee injuries
Option C is correct. This sign warns of the negative health effects of mixing cleaning supplies. Option A is not correct because the sign does not recommend conserving supplies to reduce costs. Option B is incorrect because the sign says nothing about spills. Option D is not correct because the sign does not recommend that certain cleaning supplies be used for specific tasks.

### 3. C. Call for a trained maintenance person.
Option C is correct. The images and text on the sign suggest that employees should allow a professional to repair the office machines. Options A and B are incorrect because the sign recommends that employees not attempt to fix any machines themselves. Option D is not correct because employees should call the phone number on the sign, not contact a supervisor.

### 4. B. To announce a required meeting for all employees
Option B is correct. The sign announces the date, time, location, and subject of a mandatory meeting. Its purpose is to inform employees about the meeting. Option A is incorrect because the sign's purpose is to inform, not to persuade. Option C is not correct because the meeting is mandatory, not the insurance. Option D is not correct. While the sign does inform employees that these meeting rooms will be in use, communicating this information is not the main purpose of the sign.

## Lesson 10 Test Your WRC Skills (pages 104–105)

### 1. C. You might fall off the ladder.
Option C is correct. The words and picture in the sign warn you of what might happen if you carry tools in your hand when climbing a ladder, and the sign tells you how to keep yourself safe. Option A is not correct because the sign does not suggest that anything will happen to the ladder. Option B is not correct because wearing a tool belt is not a consequence of climbing a ladder. Option D is incorrect because the sign is not about forgetting tools; it is about dropping them.

### 2. A. An early flower delivery
Option A is correct. The subject line, as well as the content of the e-mail, discusses an early flower delivery. Option B is not correct because the wedding bouquets have already been requested. Option C is incorrect because the client called to make the request. Option D is not correct because the flowers, not the wedding, need to be early.

### 3. C. Authorized personnel
Option C is correct. The title and first two sentences explain that only authorized personnel are allowed on the freight elevator. Options A and B are incorrect because tenants and guests are not allowed on the freight elevator. Option D is not correct. The sign states that building management can help arrange for large deliveries, but the sign does not address whether or not management can use the freight elevator.

### 4. D. Very satisfied
Option D is correct. The customer has marked "Very Satisfied" for four out of five items on the survey, and has written very positive comments. Options A and B are incorrect because nowhere on the survey does the customer write less than a satisfied response. Option C is incorrect because the question is looking for the customer's overall satisfaction, and the survey has many more "Very Satisfied" boxes marked than "Satisfied." In addition, the comments are very positive.

### 5. B. Bank holidays
Option B is correct. The title and content of the document explain that bank holidays will be observed, and employees will not have to work on these days. Option A is incorrect because the document provides a list of observed holidays. Option C is incorrect because Christmas is the only religious holiday on the list. Option D is incorrect because only some holidays are listed, and taking off additional days must be requested and approved.

## Chapter 3 Assessment (pages 108–109)

**1. B. Lowest**
Option B is correct. *Minimum* means lowest. The chart shows the lowest temperature each kind of meat must reach before serving. Option A is incorrect because this chart is for cooked meat, not raw meat. Option C is incorrect because the chart shows temperatures after cooking, not at the start of cooking. Option D is incorrect because the chart shows the lowest, not the highest, required internal temperature.

**2. C. You should look for another place to store your lunch.**
Option C is correct. The sign says that no food or drink should be stored in this refrigerator. Option A is incorrect because the signs says not to store food in the refrigerator. Option B is incorrect because there is no indication that anything outside the refrigerator may be contaminated. Option D is incorrect because nothing in the sign indicates that employees cannot bring their lunch to this job site.

**3. D. Yes, because the supplies are for the company.**
Option D is correct. The policy says Internet use is for company purposes. Shopping online for office supplies would be an office-related task, so it would be allowed. Option A is incorrect because employees may use the Internet for company-related purposes. Option B is incorrect because online shopping is allowed for company-related purposes. Option C is incorrect because the policy does not mention getting a supervisor's approval.

**4. C. The bonus is based on initial employment date and number of hours worked.**
Option C is correct. An employee filling out the form needs to know whether he or she was employed on the first day of the year and how many hours he or she has worked to determine the amount of his or her bonus. Options A and B are incorrect because the bonus is based on both items. Option D is incorrect because not all employees will receive the same bonus.

**5. A. Cacti and succulents**
Option A is correct. The sign says that both cacti and succulents require bright light. Options B, C, and D are incorrect because both ferns and bromeliads require medium light, which would not be found in a very sunny location.

## Lesson 11 Test Your WRC Skills (pages 118–119)

**1. D. Spend more time cleaning the bakery.**
Option D is correct. According to the survey results, customers feel that the bakery's cleanliness needs the most improvement. The biggest section of the pie chart represents comments about the cleanliness of the shop. Options A, B, and C are incorrect because value, presentation, and service represent smaller sections of the pie chart.

**2. A. Spot and Daisy**
Option A is correct. The schedule suggests that animals needing medication require more care, and Spot and Daisy need medication. Option B is incorrect because Max and Tallulah do not require medication. Option C is incorrect because only Spot requires medication. Option D is incorrect because animals that need medication require more care than those that do not.

**3. C. Cut down on waste and recycle whenever possible.**
Option C is correct because the sign reminds employees to reduce, reuse, and recycle. Option A is incorrect because the word *green* is used to indicate an environmentally friendly office, not an office with green walls. Option B is incorrect because the sign asks employees to recycle, not to start a recycling program. Option D is incorrect because the sign does not suggest that employees should monitor or report one another.

**4. D. By working hard and being eager to learn and take on more responsibility**
Option D is correct. The third sentence in the e-mail explains that these qualities helped Rachel earn the promotion. Option A is incorrect because the e-mail does not reference a test. Option B is incorrect because working for three years with the company isn't the main reason Rachel earned a promotion. Option C is incorrect because Rachel hasn't started training customer service representatives yet.

**5. C. Experienced employees who wish to learn more about managing**
Option C is correct. The *Managing Workflow* training course is aimed at employees who wish to learn more about management. Option A is incorrect because employees must gain experience on the job before moving up to the role of manager. Option B is incorrect because employees must use their knowledge on the job before managing others. Option D is incorrect because employees with no construction experience should take *Knowing the Basics*.

## Lesson 12 Test Your WRC Skills (pages 126–127)

**1. A. It protects workers by making them more noticeable to drivers.**

Option A is correct. The sign says that workers must wear high visibility clothing. This means that the clothing can be easily seen by others. The reason, or effect, of the sign is to provide safety for the workers since they will be working on a highway with cars driving by. Option B is incorrect because highway workers generally do not wear professional clothing. Option C is incorrect because the workers know they are at work and will see the sign at the work site. Option D is incorrect because the sign tells workers what to wear, not drivers what to do.

**2. C. The supervisor will tell the employee to cover the tattoo.**

Option C is correct. The first effect of an employee not covering his or her tattoos is that the employee will receive a verbal warning, which means that he or she will be told to cover the tattoos. Options A and B are incorrect because these consequences will only happen if the verbal warning is ignored. Option D is incorrect because the employee will not be fired as a first disciplinary measure.

**3. B. It will be sent back to be smoothed.**

Option B is correct. If a clock face fails inspection (the cause), it will be sent back to be smoothed (effect). The "Fail" arrow in the flow chart indicates this answer. Option A is incorrect because the flow chart does not mention anything about throwing the clock face away. Option C is not correct. The "Fail" arrow on the flow chart does not point back to the first step of the production process. Option D is not correct because moving to the next step is what happens if a clock face passes inspection.

**4. D. The restaurant gets the most business on Saturdays.**

Option D is correct. The graph shows that the restaurant gets the most customers on Saturdays. The result is that the manager likely needs more help on this day of the week. Option A is incorrect because the graph does not explain why more customers come in on Saturdays. Option B is incorrect because Saturdays get the most customers, not the least. Option C is incorrect because nothing is mentioned on the graph about the manager's availability to work on certain days.

**5. A. The vet does not want to expose boarded pets to sick animals.**

Option A is correct. The document states that the reason for the proof of vaccinations and no-parasite policy is to ensure the safety and health of the animals. You can infer that if a sick animal is boarded (cause), it might make the other animals sick (effect). Options B, C, and D are incorrect because nothing is implied in the policy about lack of money, time, or trust at the vet's office.

## Lesson 13 Test Your WRC Skills (pages 134–135)

**1. C. HVAC Technician**

Option C is correct. Someone who wants to get a job fixing air conditioning systems in cars should enroll in Community College's HVAC Technician program. The third row in the "Brief Overview" column explains that air conditioning systems are covered in the HVAC Technician program. Option A is incorrect because Community College's Commercial Electrician program is about installations in commercial buildings, not air conditioning systems in cars. Option B is incorrect because the Residential Electrician program is about installations in homes, not cars. Option D is incorrect because the Electrical Engineer/Aviation program is about electronic systems in planes, not cars.

**2. C. Sun Mountain**

Option C is correct. Employees should recommend Sun Mountain to customers who have never skied before. The trail guide states that Sun Mountain is a beginner slope. Option A is incorrect because Sky Mountain I has dangerous terrain and is for experienced skiers only. Option B is incorrect because the trail guide says Sky Mountain II is for advanced skiers only. Option D is incorrect because the trail guide states that Mountain Peak is an intermediate slope, not a beginner slope.

**3. A. Ad writers**

Option A is correct. The ad writers have the longest training. The e-mail states that ad writers have six days of training. Option B is incorrect because the e-mail says sales personnel have four days of training. Options C and D are incorrect because the design team and telemarketers have only one day of training.

**4. D. EMT 4**

Option D is correct. According to the chart, EMT 4s can perform the highest level of emergency care. Options A, B, and C are incorrect because EMT levels 1, 2, and 3 may not give oral and intravenous drugs, but EMT 4s may perform these duties.

**5. B. Boys' outerwear**

Option B is correct. Sales in the boys' outerwear department went up 10%. Option A is incorrect because sales in the girls' outerwear department went up 7%, which is less than 10%. Option C is incorrect because sales in the girls' shoe department did not rise; they went down 2%. Option D is incorrect because sales in the boys' shoe department went up 6%, which is less than the 10% rise in the boys' outerwear department.

## Chapter 4 Assessment (pages 138–139)

**1. A. Employees with young children**
Option A is correct. According to the notice, employees with children under 12 years old would enroll in the program. Option B is incorrect because employees with no children would not need day care. Option C is incorrect because the day care is only for children under 12 years old. Option D is incorrect because the notice says the day care costs $350 per month.

**2. C. Large arrangements require vases at least 5 inches wide at the base.**
Option C is correct. The instructions say that employees should choose a vase at least 5 inches wide at the base for large arrangements. Option A is incorrect because small, not large, arrangements go in vases less than 5 inches wide. Option B is incorrect because the instructions say to use filler and greenery in both small and large arrangements. Option D is incorrect because the instructions say to use large flowers for large arrangements, not small or medium flowers.

**3. C. Customer satisfaction and the average purchase amount both increased.**
Option C is correct. The graph shows that customer satisfaction and average purchase amount both increased. Option A is incorrect because customer satisfaction increased, not decreased. Option B is incorrect because the percentage of first-time customers who returned to the store increased, not decreased. Option D is incorrect because the average purchase amount increased, not stayed the same.

**4. B. Jared should learn ways to reduce errors.**
Option B is correct. The evaluator writes that Jared could strive for improvement in reducing errors. Option A is incorrect because the evaluator doesn't mention how well Jared gets along with other employees. Options C and D are incorrect because the evaluator writes that Jared has good attendance and has learned the procedures for completing his job.

**5. D. Sales representatives will be assigned suburban communities to target.**
Option D is correct. The e-mail discusses a new initiative to increase sales in suburban areas. The reader can infer that the sales representatives will be asked to target new suburban areas. Option A is incorrect because the meeting is about a new, not old, sales initiative. Option B is incorrect because the e-mail does not mention Human Resources or salary changes. Option C is incorrect because the e-mail says the sales department will be targeting suburban, not urban, areas.

## Lesson 14 Test Your WRC Skills (pages 148–149)

**1. B. Good Sport Sporting Goods**
Option B is correct. Lakisha must apply her prior knowledge (that a basketball is sports equipment) and then read the mall floor plan to identify a store that sells sports equipment. She can use the names of the stores to infer what they sell. Of the stores in the mall, Lakisha will most likely recommend Good Sport Sporting Goods because the name implies that it sells sports equipment. Option A is incorrect because it is a shoe store. Option C is incorrect because it is a beauty salon. Option D is incorrect because an apparel store sells clothing, not sporting goods.

**2. D. $15.00**
Option D is correct. You already know that a prom gown is a type of fancy dress, and you can use the price list to identify how much a fancy dress costs to dry clean ($15.00). Option A is incorrect because a prom gown is not a shirt, which costs $5.00 to be cleaned. Option B is not correct because a prom gown is not a sweater, skirt, or pair of pants, all of which cost $6.00 to be cleaned. Option C is incorrect because $10.00 is the cost to dry clean a casual dress, not a fancy dress.

**3. D. He must complete the Medical Records Release Form.**
Option D is correct. You need to use your prior knowledge that the patient is 8 years old, and therefore a minor. According to the policy, the guardian (in this case, the father) must fill out the Medical Records Release Form to transfer his daughter's medical records. Option A is not correct because the daughter is too young to fill out her own release form. Options B and C are incorrect because neither the school nurse nor the doctor need to fill out the Medical Records Release Form.

**4. A. 12**
Option A is correct. When you read the report, you must apply your prior knowledge that beverages are drinks, and soda is a kind of drink. Options B, C, and D are incorrect because they indicate the number of cases of non-beverage items that were delivered to the convenience store.

**5. C. Place the consumer's information on the internal "No-Call List."**
Option C is correct. Milo must already understand that hanging up on somebody shows a lack of interest. He must apply this knowledge to the instruction in the memo to place consumers who show lack of interest on the internal "No-Call List." Option A is incorrect because Milo should only contact his manager with questions. Option B is incorrect because the memo states that nonverbal lack of interest by a consumer means he or she should be placed on the "No-Call List," and therefore not contacted again. Option D is not correct because even though the consumer didn't actually say not to call again, his actions clearly showed a lack of interest in the solicitation.

## Lesson 15 Test Your WRC Skills (pages 156–157)

**1. C. Sweet potatoes**
Option C is correct. The scenario indicates that the recipient of the memo works in the produce department, and sweet potatoes are the only item listed from the produce department. Options A, B, and D are incorrect because these items are not found in the produce department. The other departments addressed in the memo will need to adjust the prices on these items.

**2. A. Take responsibility for the safety of your work environment.**
Option A is correct. The text emphasizes that all employees are responsible for workplace safety. This idea is also represented in the pie chart, in which messy work stations and failure to wear safety equipment are the top causes of workplace accidents. Option B is incorrect because the notice asks employees to help reduce workplace injuries, which is a good reason to follow the rules. Option C is incorrect because a safe workplace is the main idea of the notice, not an attractive workplace. Option D is incorrect because the document says that workplace injuries are uncommon. The pie chart does not tell the number of accidents; it only divides them into three causes.

**3. B. Prime the wall with an oil-based primer.**
Option B is correct because the document warns painters that problems will result if they do not prime oil-based surfaces with oil-based primer before covering with water-based paint. Option A is incorrect because peeling is what happens when the wall is not properly primed. Option C is incorrect because priming over peeling paint is not a situation that the document addresses. Option D is incorrect because the document specifically instructs painters to use oil-based primer.

**4. D. Recommend model 947623 and offer a 10% discount.**
Option D is correct. The tire cannot be repaired and there are no tires with the same model number in stock. The warranty note tells employees what to do in this situation. Option A is incorrect because employees are instructed to recommend a comparable model. Option B is incorrect because the tire cannot be repaired. Option C is incorrect because these models are not the most comparable to model 940614.

**5. B. Explain that the offer is valid only with a new purchase.**
Option B is correct. The policy says that the offer is valid only with a new purchase, and this customer is not making a new purchase. Option A is incorrect because the customer has not made a new purchase and does not qualify for the offer. Option C is incorrect because the policy does not say anything about inspecting a customer's jewelry. Option D is incorrect because the sign clearly states that the offer is good only on new purchases, not purchases made a year ago.

## Chapter 5 Assessment (pages 160–161)

**1. B. The item is 20% off.**
Option B is correct. A cat brush is a grooming supply. The chart shows that all grooming supplies in the cat department are 20% off. Option A is incorrect because no items are 10% off. Option C is incorrect because grooming supplies for dogs, not cats, are 30% off. Option D is incorrect because the chart shows that grooming supplies for cats are on sale.

**2. D. Explain that the customer may use one coupon.**
Option D is correct. Value Dollar's price-match guarantee states that competitors' coupons are accepted. The sign also says that there is a limit of one coupon per purchase. Option A is incorrect because customers can use competitors' coupons at Value Store, and Grocery Mart is a competitor. Option B is incorrect because the sign says only one coupon may be used per item. Option C is incorrect because nothing in the situation suggests that the customer's coupons are expired.

**3. A. Call a manager for assistance and try to restart the cash register.**
Option A is correct. If your register is not working, the best thing to do is to call a manager and try to get your register to come on again. Option B is incorrect. Although this option keeps the customer from being inconvenienced, the store and your manager would probably not approve of this solution. Option C is incorrect because you would not be able to do these things if the register is not working. Option D is incorrect because it would greatly inconvenience the customer.

**4. C. Send an apology e-mail with a coupon for a new pair of shoes.**
Option C is correct. In this situation, it would be most appropriate to send an apology with a coupon for a new pair of shoes. Option A is incorrect because you should address the complaint, not try to pass it off on someone else. Option B is incorrect because the shoes should last beyond one wearing, even if they were purchased at an outlet store. Option D is incorrect because it inconveniences the customer and does not constitute excellent customer service.

**5. D. Parking Garage A, Level 2**
Option D is correct. The notice tells you that Parking Garage B will be closed and asks non-disabled employees to avoid parking on Level 1 of Parking Garage A. Options A and B are incorrect because Parking Garage B will be undergoing repairs. Option C is incorrect because it would not be considerate of the disabled employees who work in the building and need those parking spaces.